Martha's Vineyard
Seasons

A Photographic Essay by Paul Rezendes

Section Introductions by Tony Omer

Tide-mark Press, Ltd.
East Hartford, Connecticut

Published by Tide-mark Press, Ltd.
22 Prestige Park Circle, East Hartford, Connecticut 06108-1917

Text design and map by Dan Veale/AMV Graphics

ISBN 1-59490-113-9

Library of Congress Control Number: 2005924656

Second Edition/First Printing

Printed in Korea

Contents

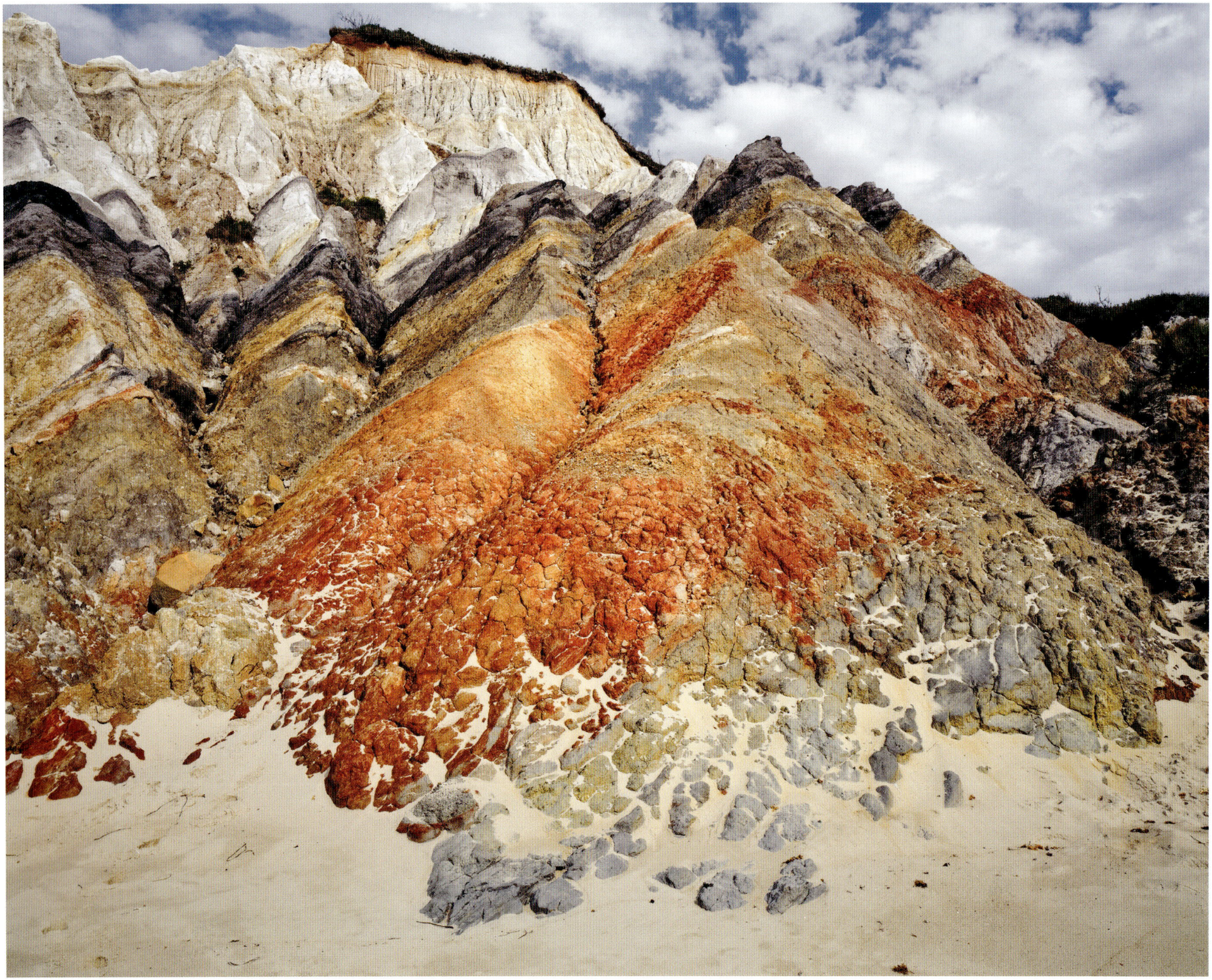

Gay Head Cliffs Aquinnah

Paul Rezendes on the Vineyard

My first trips to Martha's Vineyard were prompted by reasons very different from those of most visitors to the island. At the time of my first trip in November 1988, I made my living as a professional wildlife tracker, consultant, and photographer. My wife, Paulette Roy, and I owned and operated a school that specialized in teaching people how to read animal tracks and sign. After learning that there were many skunks and turkeys (the wild, feathered variety) on the island, I set out to photograph turkeys and to document the skunk sign. The turkeys roosted and foraged at Massachusetts Audubon's Felix Neck Wildlife Sanctuary. The birds had grown accustomed to people, and so they allowed me to approach them quite closely, which made for some great photo opportunities. The shooting was so productive that I revisited the island several times during the next few years to augment my stock of wildlife photographs. (At the time of this writing in 2005, the staff at Felix Neck reports that the turkeys, although still on the island, no longer inhabit their grounds.)

In the early 1990s, while continuing to photograph the turkeys, I began to explore the island farther afield, experimenting with small-format 35mm landscape images. Eventually my interest shifted from wildlife to scenic landscapes, and as my photography business expanded, a small client base developed who were interested in Martha's Vineyard images for a variety of projects.

I didn't get really serious about Martha's Vineyard landscape photography, however, until December 1994. That month, I packed my van and ferried to the island, fully equipped with my medium- and large-format cameras, lenses, and assorted photography paraphernalia, much more equipment than anyone could physically carry at one time. My photographic equipment far outweighed my personal gear! One landscape-only "shoot" with my large-format camera, and I was hooked! Thus began a photographic love affair with the island that has evolved into two or more photographic expeditions every year. Coincidentally, my youngest daughter, Lianna, was discovering and falling in love with the island herself at about the same time, allowing me a place to stay. In 2001, I purchased a sailboat, which has become a great platform from which to pursue photography. I now make it a point to explore the island from the dual perspectives of land and sea.

I'm fortunate to have the sort of job that requires me to travel through New England seeking out the beauty it has to offer. To me, Martha's Vineyard is diversity at its copious best: villages, forests, coastal plains, beaches, marshes, ponds, ocean-side cliffs, lighthouses, harbors, and an island connected to the island. Those diverse habitats invite exploration by visitors, islanders, and photographers alike. From the colorful gingerbread houses in Oak Bluffs that would be at home in Candyland, to the Gay Head Cliffs in Aquinnah, with multihued clays and rocks that appear to melt into the Atlantic Ocean (sometimes coloring it red at the shoreline), there is a vast amount to see and experience. The harbors have personalities as varied as the island's towns. Secluded, lesser-known Lake Tashmoo contrasts dramatically with the active harbors at Edgartown and Oak Bluffs. Vineyard Haven Harbor, graced by classic wooden schooners, feels far different from the working harbor in Menemsha with its mix of fishing trawlers and recreational yachts, power and sail alike. Rich in history and marine lore, the island also hosts five lighthouses: East Chop, West Chop, Edgartown, Cape Poge, and Gay Head.

Each season on the island offers its own palette of colors, each village its own unique flavor, each harbor its own scent of the sea. No matter how many times I visit Martha's Vineyard, the elements, natural and manmade, continually swirl into a kaleidoscope of new and ever-changing scenes. It's a photographer's business not to miss much, but I know that for me the island still abounds with photographic potential, unborn images awaiting discovery, capture, and release. Plan to see me around ... just look for the guy behind the tripod, under the black cloth!

Paul Rezendes

A Vineyard State of Mind

Martha's Vineyard is a home away from home for many. It is a retreat from the hectic, often mundane life of the big city. It is a trip back in time—just a little bit back, because it is not uncomfortably removed from all the conveniences of modernity. This book shows in brilliant images much of what is sought on the Vineyard: the solitude of its pristine beaches and the quiet peacefulness of woods and wetlands whose most frequent visitors are the deer and screech owls, the shorebirds, and red-tailed hawks. There are boats of pleasure dotting the harbors in summer, centerpieces of a table set for the pursuit of reflection and for the regeneration of emotional and spiritual batteries. Even the buildings in the 19th-century resort town of Oak Bluffs share their colorful playfulness. Most appropriately, the lighthouses—beacons that still help guide mariners past the island's most treacherous points—now also help guide us back to the friendliness and peacefulness that is Martha's Vineyard.

Martha's Vineyard Island is a moraine, a pile of glacial rubble. Tens of thousands of years ago, during the last Ice Age, the accumulation of snowfalls pushed a glacier down from the northernmost reaches of our planet to what are now Cape Cod and the islands. The ice rolled, grinding rock from farther north into clay, sand, and gravel, even smoothing and rounding vast boulders as it inched ahead. Some 12,000 years ago, the Earth's climate began to warm. The continental glacier slowly receded toward the polar ice cap. As the Earth warmed, the detritus left by the ice created Cape Cod, the Elizabeth Islands, Block Island, Long Island, and the islands of Nantucket and Martha's Vineyard. The deposits of sand, clay, and gravel—so much a part of our beaches—connect us directly to our geological history. The smoothly rounded rocks and boulders that lie indiscriminately over and under the land are there because of that glacier. Impediments to plowing, the rocks were gathered by farmers clearing their fields and shaped into the many stone walls that still checker the Vineyard. One can almost envision glacial melt flowing from the ice through rock and rubble to form the outwash plains that lead to the south shore and the tidal ponds, among the Vineyard's most characteristic features.

The glacial melting was not a smooth process but one that progressed in an irregular rhythm. Striations of sediment were deposited. Some of those colorful layers are revealed by the sea's erosion at Gay Head Cliffs, in the town of Aquinnah, at the westernmost point on the island. Kettle holes, left by pockets of ice that melted after the glacier retreated, were the beginnings of most of the freshwater ponds, sinkholes, and other depressions on the Vineyard.

The origin of the name "Martha's Vineyard" is not known. The Vineyard was almost as frequently referred to as "Martin's Vineyard" as late as the 18th century. Some accounts attribute the European discovery of the island to Bartholomew Gosnold, an English adventurer and trader. The same Gosnold contributed to the limited success of the Jamestown colony. While certainly not the first European in the area, Gosnold investigated a number of the local islands, including the Vineyard, during his 1602 voyage. Eventually he attempted to settle on Cuttyhunk, which he called Elizabeth's Island. He is reputed to have named Nomans Island, a 628-acre island located approximately 2.5 miles south of the Vineyard,

Martha's Island. Some say the accounts in his ship's logs inspired William Shakespeare when he wrote *The Tempest* in about 1609.

Members of the Wampanoag Native American group met Gosnold's party at several of his stops. All the accounts describe peaceful encounters. As many as 3,000 Wampanoags may have been living on the Vineyard at this time. While there was never outright warfare between the first islanders and the first off-islanders, the Native American population declined to less than a third of its numbers by the beginning of the 18th century due to disease and emigration.

Vineyard history has been characterized by dualities. During almost every period since the arrival of the Europeans, there have been at least two major groups with conflicting interests. First, there were the Wampanoags and the Europeans. Then, for several hundred years, it was the land-based agrarian community versus the sea-focused community of fishermen, whalers, and sailing folk. These divisions have shaped the current political landscape of the island. In 1892 West Tisbury broke free from Tisbury largely due to this division of interests.

The harbor towns grew as their singular interests dictated. Edgartown was a whaling center. Oak Bluffs became the location for the Methodist Camp Meeting. Vineyard Haven served as a general port town for sailing freighters. Today, Edgartown is known for its white painted homes built for whaling captains. Oak Bluffs, the old Cottage City, is the port where ferries from the mainland still deliver loads of summer people. The primary year-round port of Vineyard Haven (Tisbury) remains a harbor of refuge for mariners during bad weather, as it was for the sailing ships that once carried freight through the Vineyard Sound.

Just a few decades ago, the major division was between islanders and off-islanders. Summer people, and most anyone not born on the Vineyard, were considered off-islanders, even if they lived on the island all year. Since the 1960s, however, the infusion of off-islanders who have become year-rounders has led to a muddling of the native-islander and off-islander distinction. Today the dichotomy seems to be between year-round people and those who visit only in the summer. The Wampanoags are now a recognized tribe. Many "transplants" or "wash-a-shores" are now raising their families here, including most recently a significant number of Brazilian immigrants.

Most Vineyarders, whether year-rounders or summer people, only recognize two states of being: on-island and off-island. Just a few years ago, a very young Vineyarder, when asked where she had been after returning from a three-week European vacation with her family, replied quite innocently, "Off-island." *America, over there, the real world, the mainland:* those are all terms used to describe what all Vineyarders would recognize as *off-island*. We like to think the island is unique. Most islanders do not think of the Vineyard as a microcosm, although there may be some interesting similarities with life in other places. Instead, they prefer to see it as a completely different set of relationships within a different socioeconomic reality. At the very least, the Vineyard is certainly a singular state of mind—a Vineyard state of mind.

Tony Omer

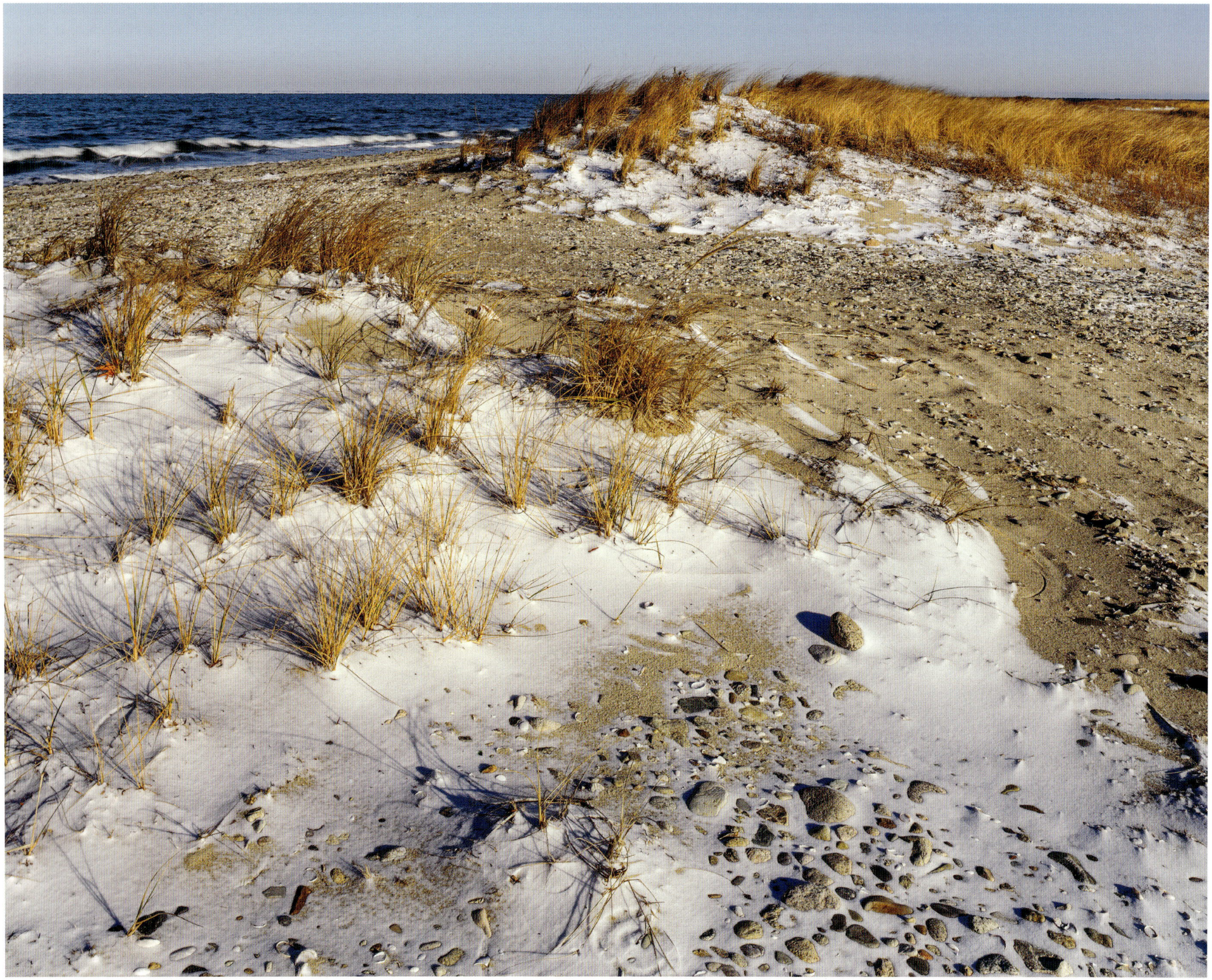

Winter White

Cape Poge Wildlife Refuge, Chappaquiddick

✦WINTER✦

IT IS A RITE OF PASSAGE — THE INITIATION THAT COMES from living through the winter here makes a true Vineyarder. After summer and fall, it is the abrupt transformation in Vineyard life that seems so unnerving. There are evenings when only one or two cars pass as you drive through the entire island. A walk along a beach may be made wholly alone, without ever seeing another soul. It does not get quite so cold as in other parts of New England, and the snowfalls are generally moderate. The silence of long dark nights, broken only by the sounds of wind and rain beating on the panes, and accompanied by days of endless gray winter skies, gives one pause.

Vineyarders have strategies for coping. They talk with neighbors over their mail at the post office. Cutting and stacking firewood is useful, and there is endless planning—if not always completion—of those activities that there wasn't time for during the rest of the year. Town politics is a time-honored preoccupation. There are strings of committee meetings and the all-important town meetings. The libraries are open and there are book groups, in addition to the community chorus, community theater, and a host of more typical New England winter pastimes. Winter is vacation time for most Vineyarders. The schools' winter vacation schedules are even set up to avoid those of off-island schools. Then it's often skiing or off to warmer spots down south. Spring is just around the bend. We can wait.

— *T.O.*

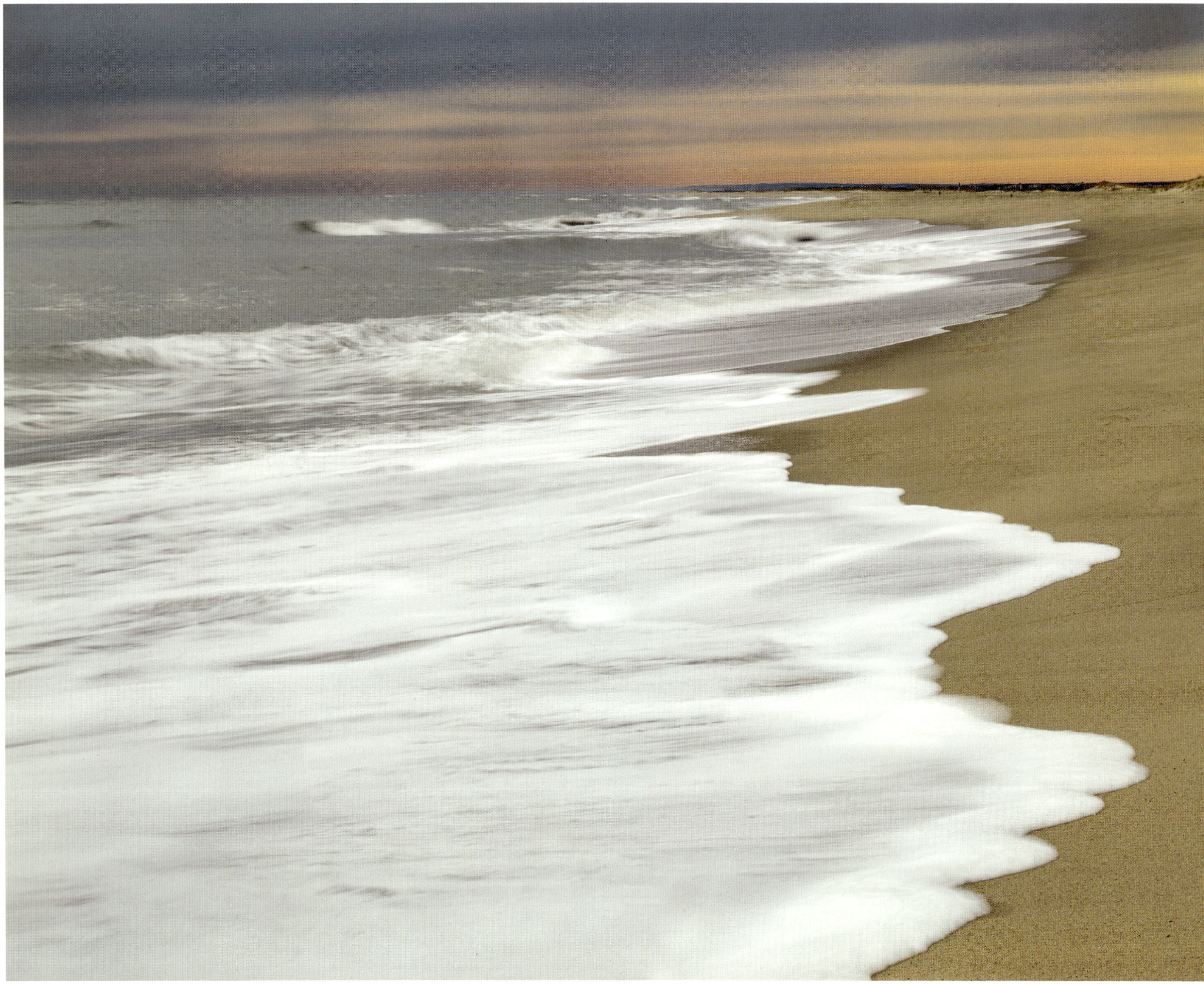

Surf Swept Shore

Wasque Wildlife Refuge, Chappaquiddick

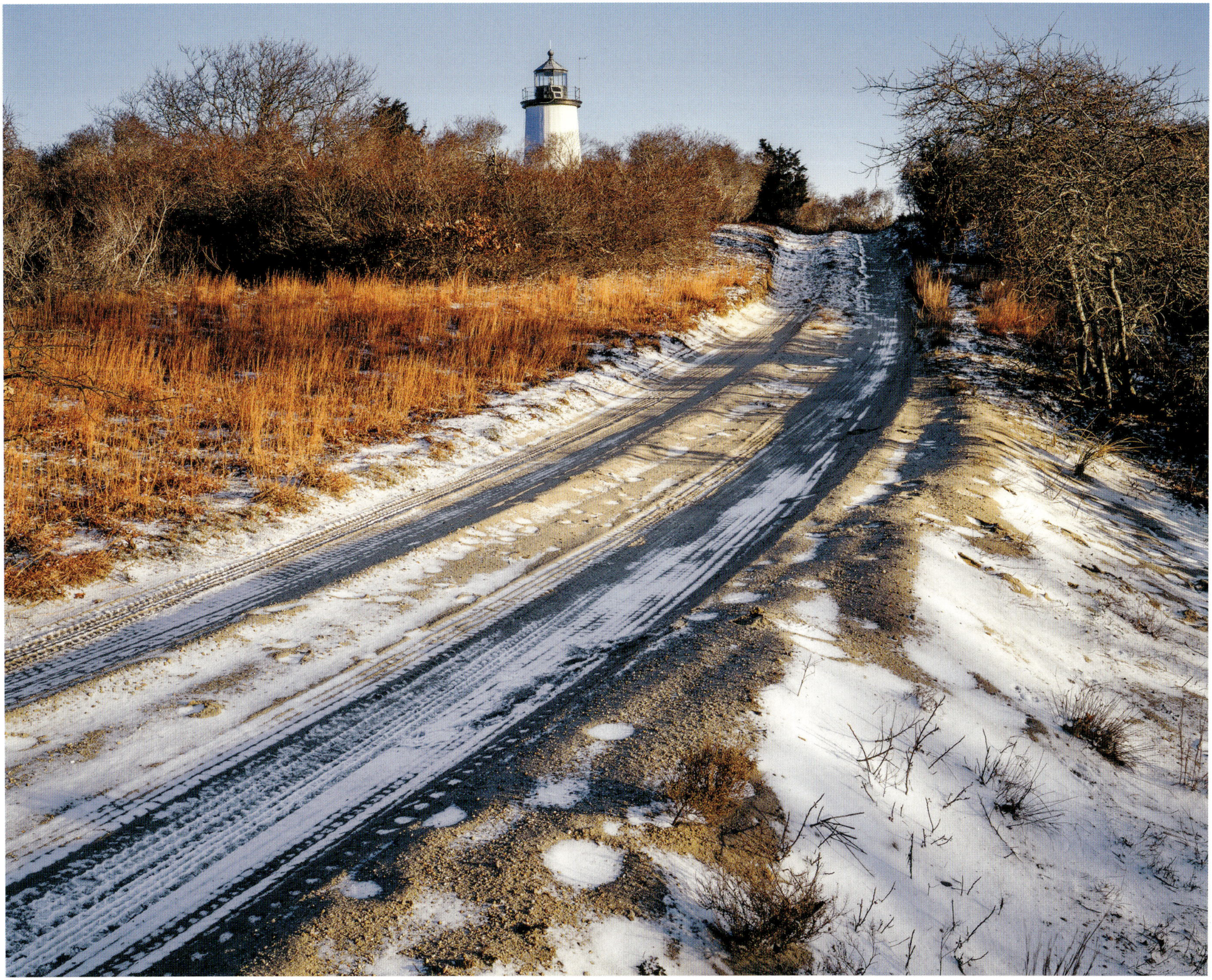

Snow at Cape Poge Light

Chappaquiddick

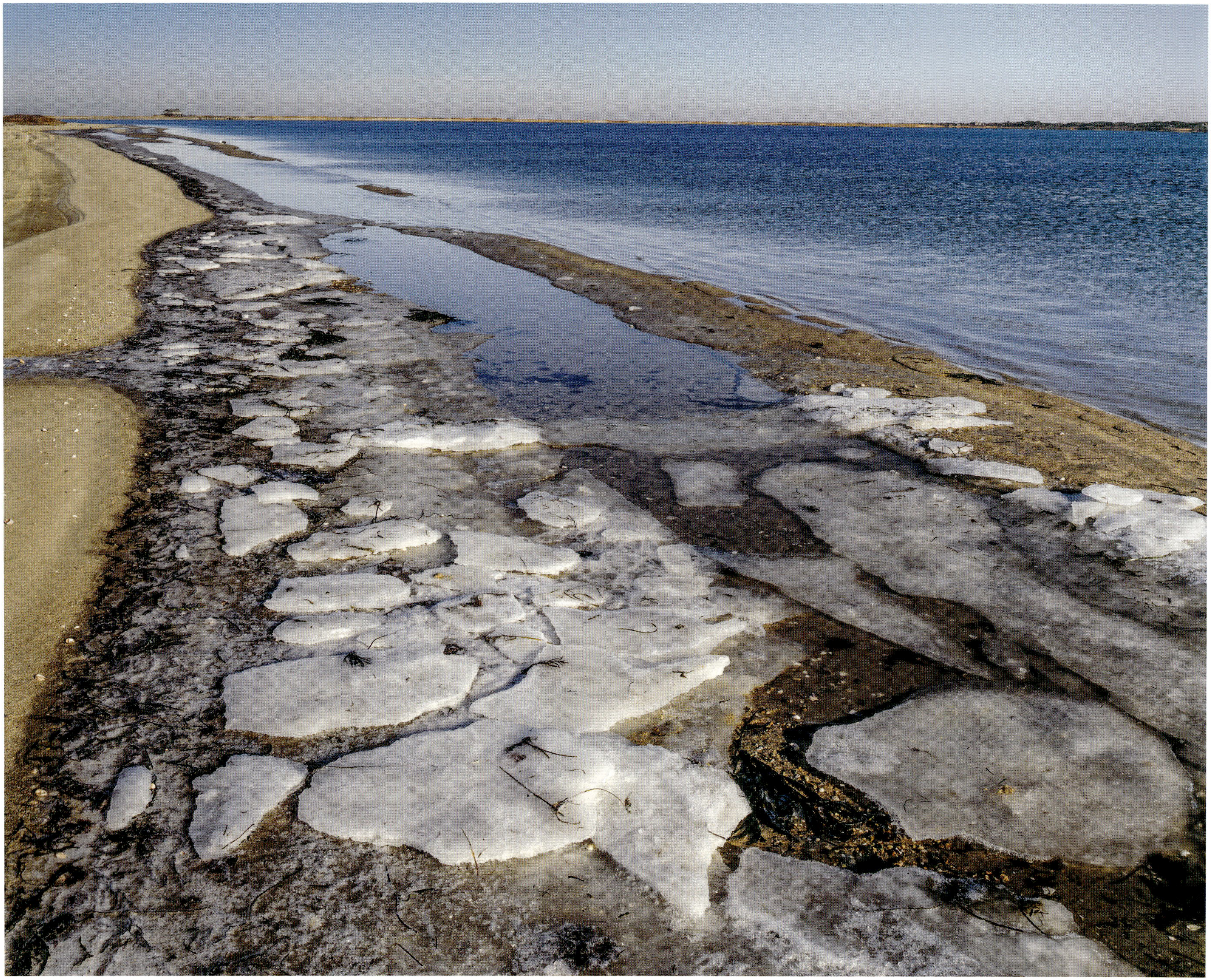

Ice-rimmed Bay

Cape Poge Wildlife Refuge, Chappaquiddick

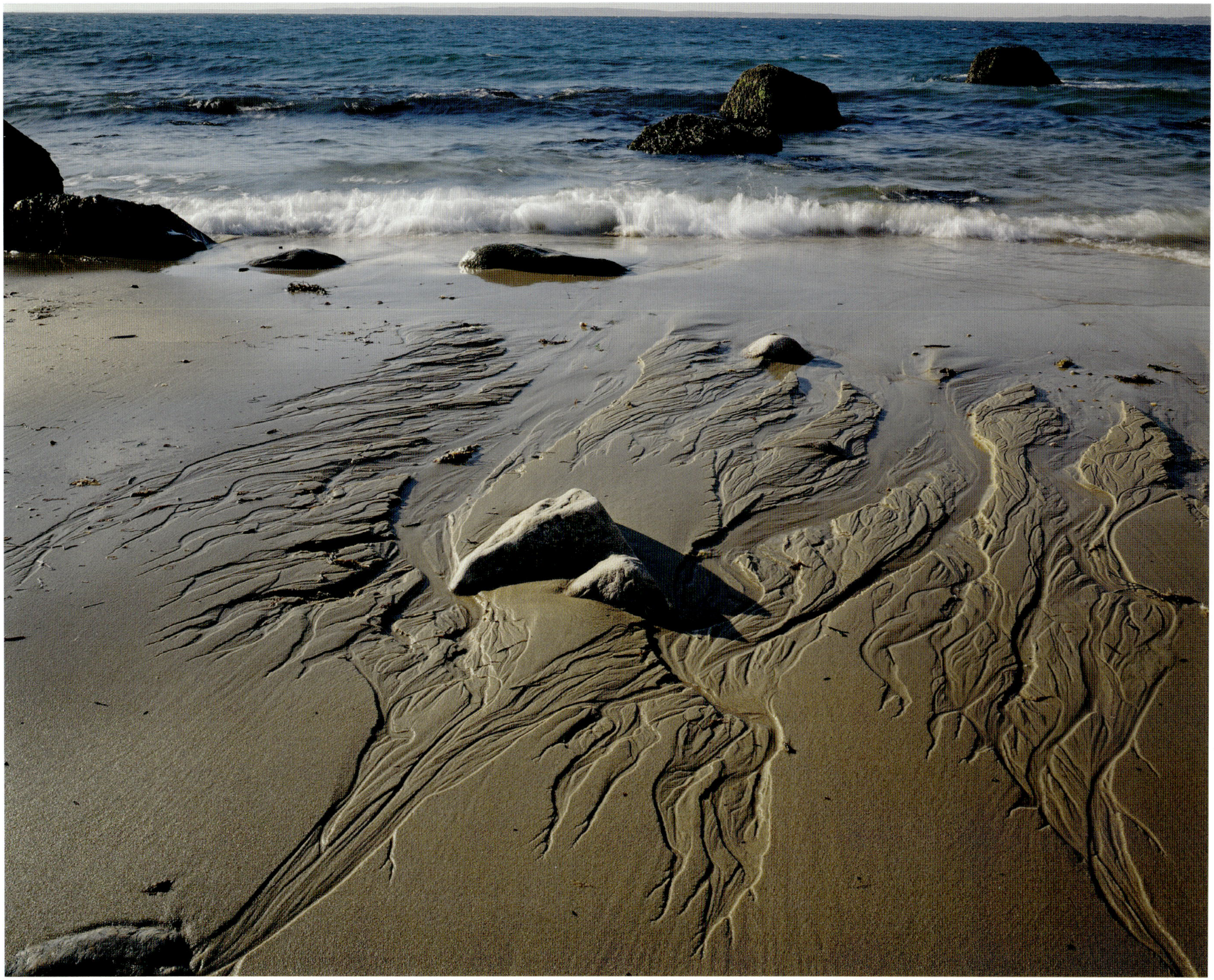

Sand Creatures   Cedar Tree Neck, West Tisbury

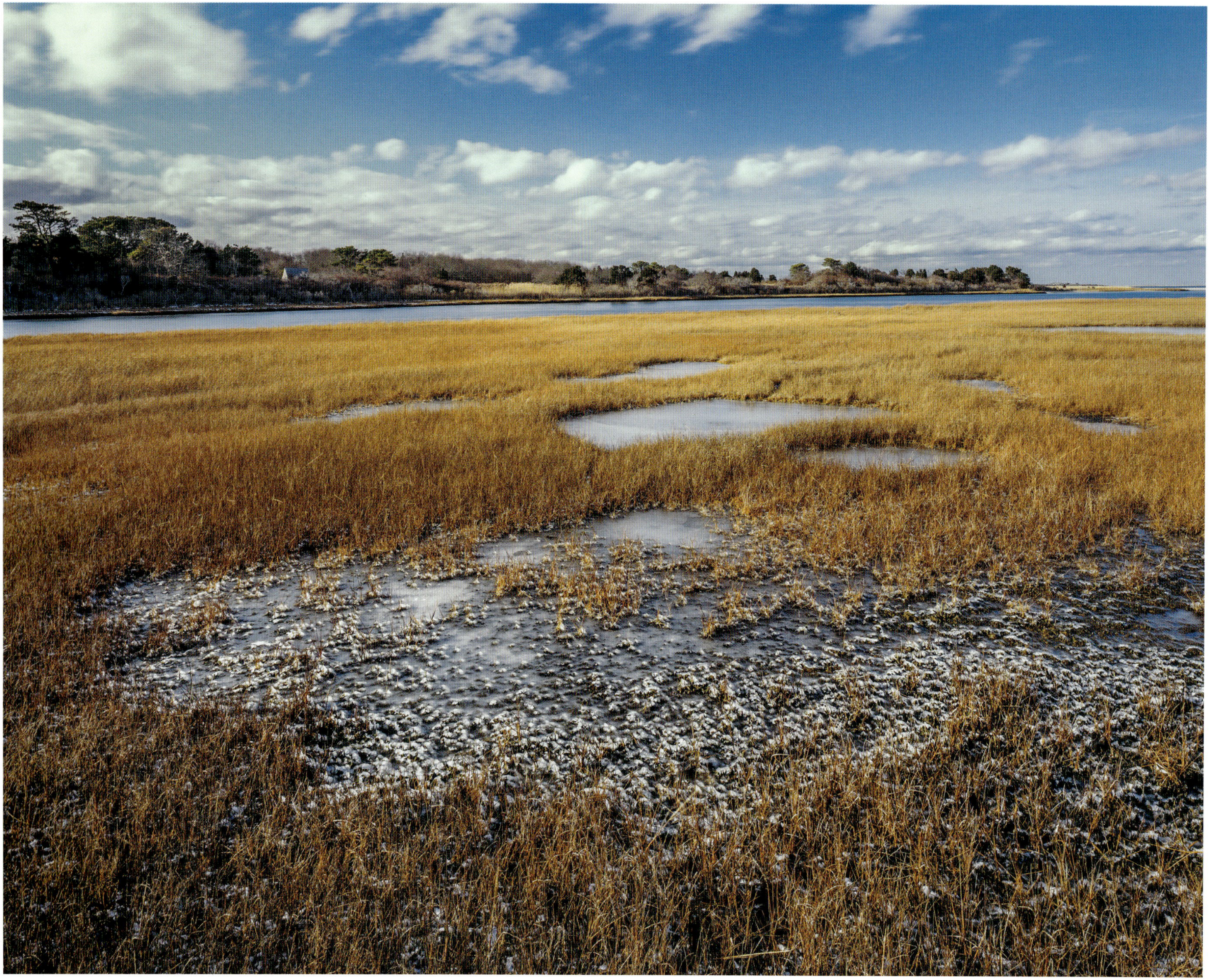

Frozen Salt Marsh

Cape Poge Bay and Tomo Neck, Chappaquiddick

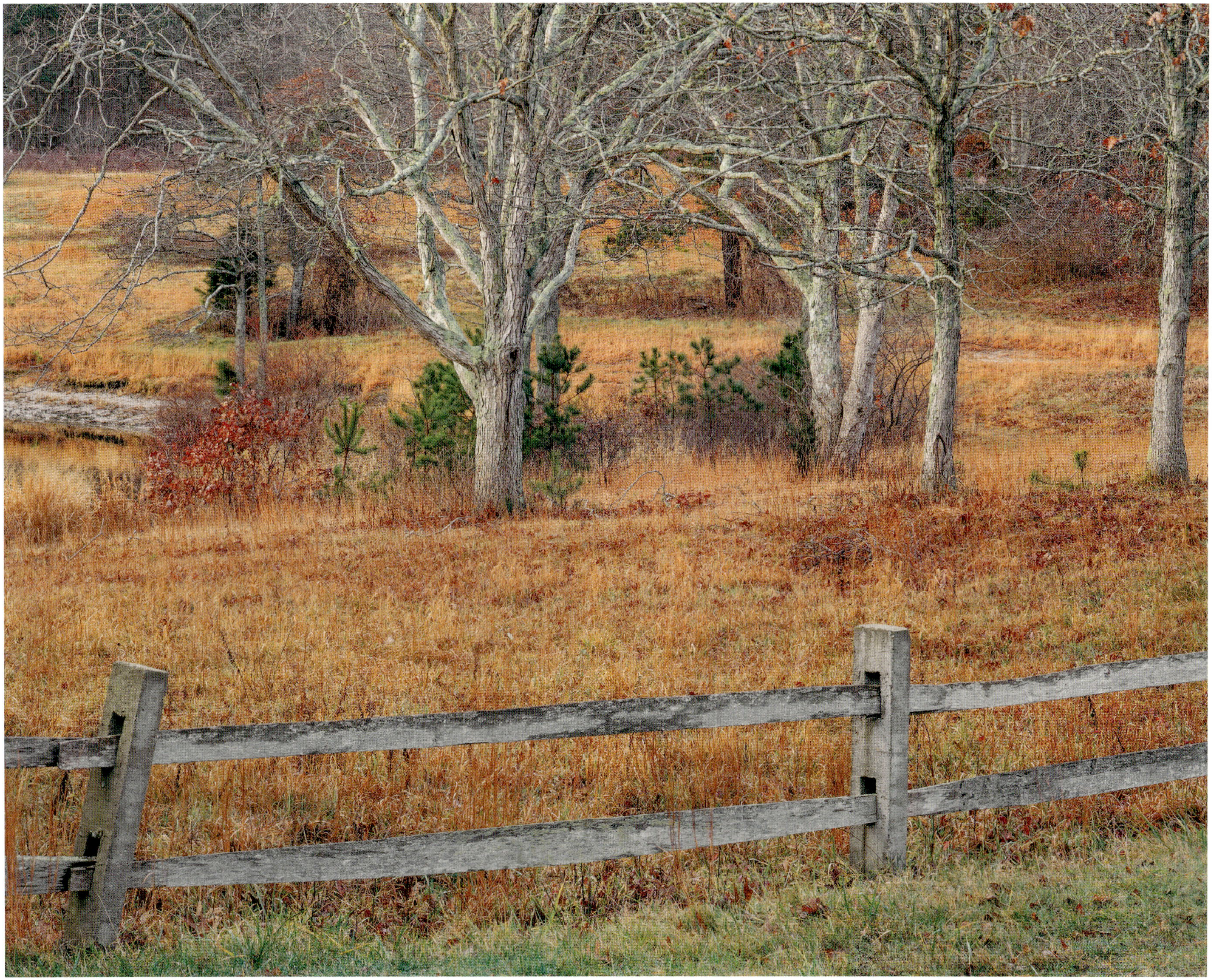

The Meadow at Brine's Pond — Chappaquiddick

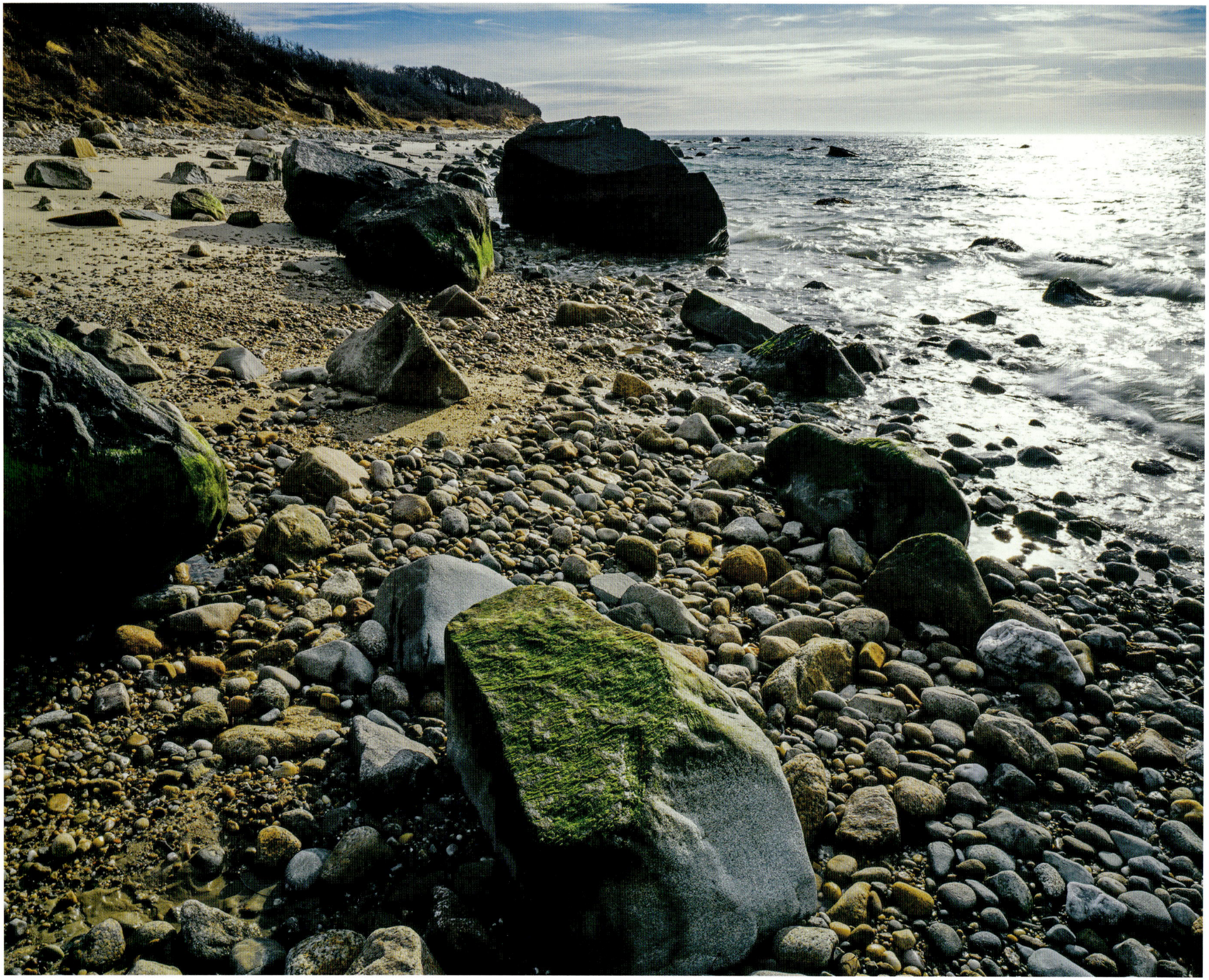

Stony Beach

Cedar Tree Neck, West Tisbury

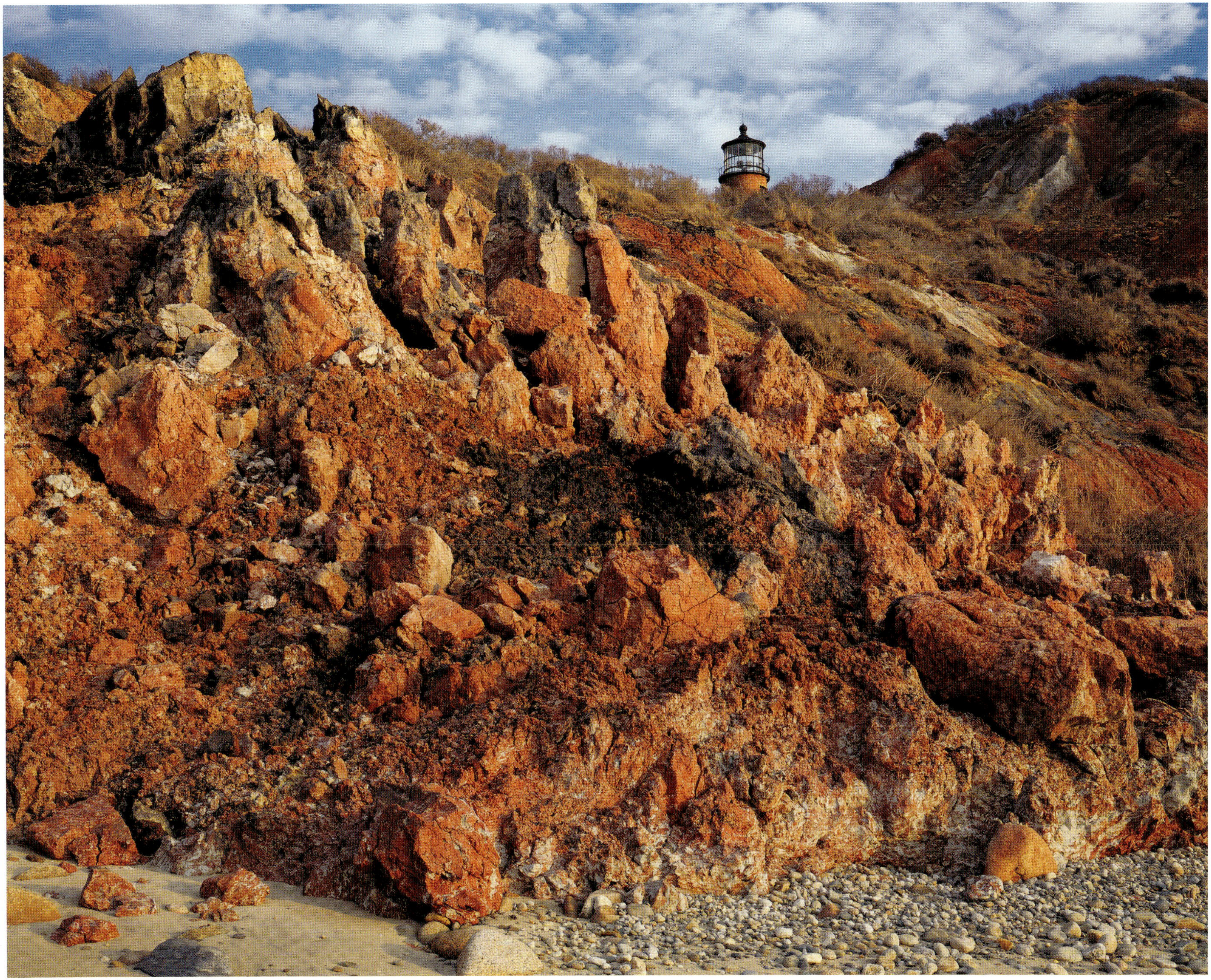

Winter Edged Cliffs

Gay Head Cliffs, Aquinnah

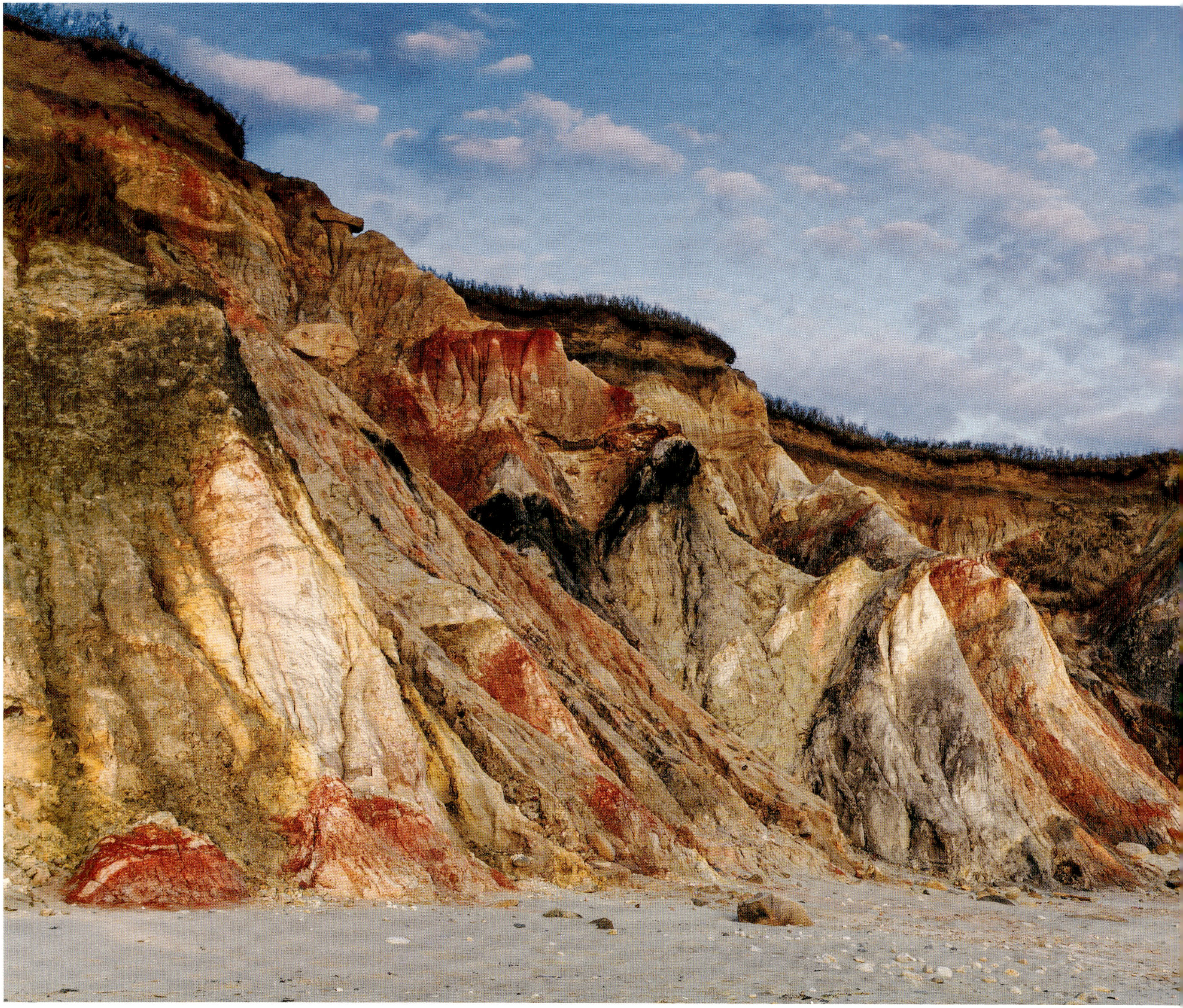

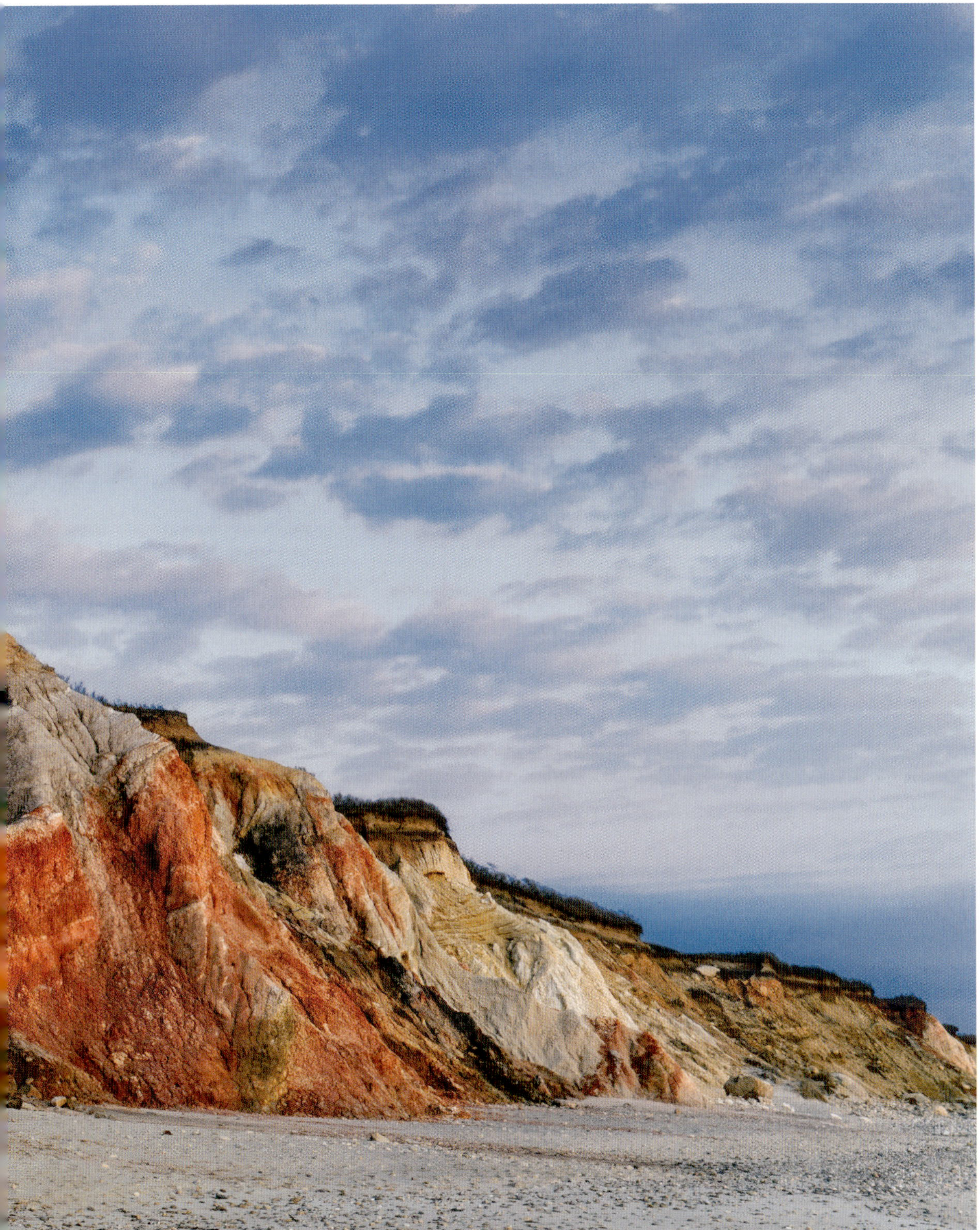

Empty Shore

Gay Head Cliffs,
Aquinnah

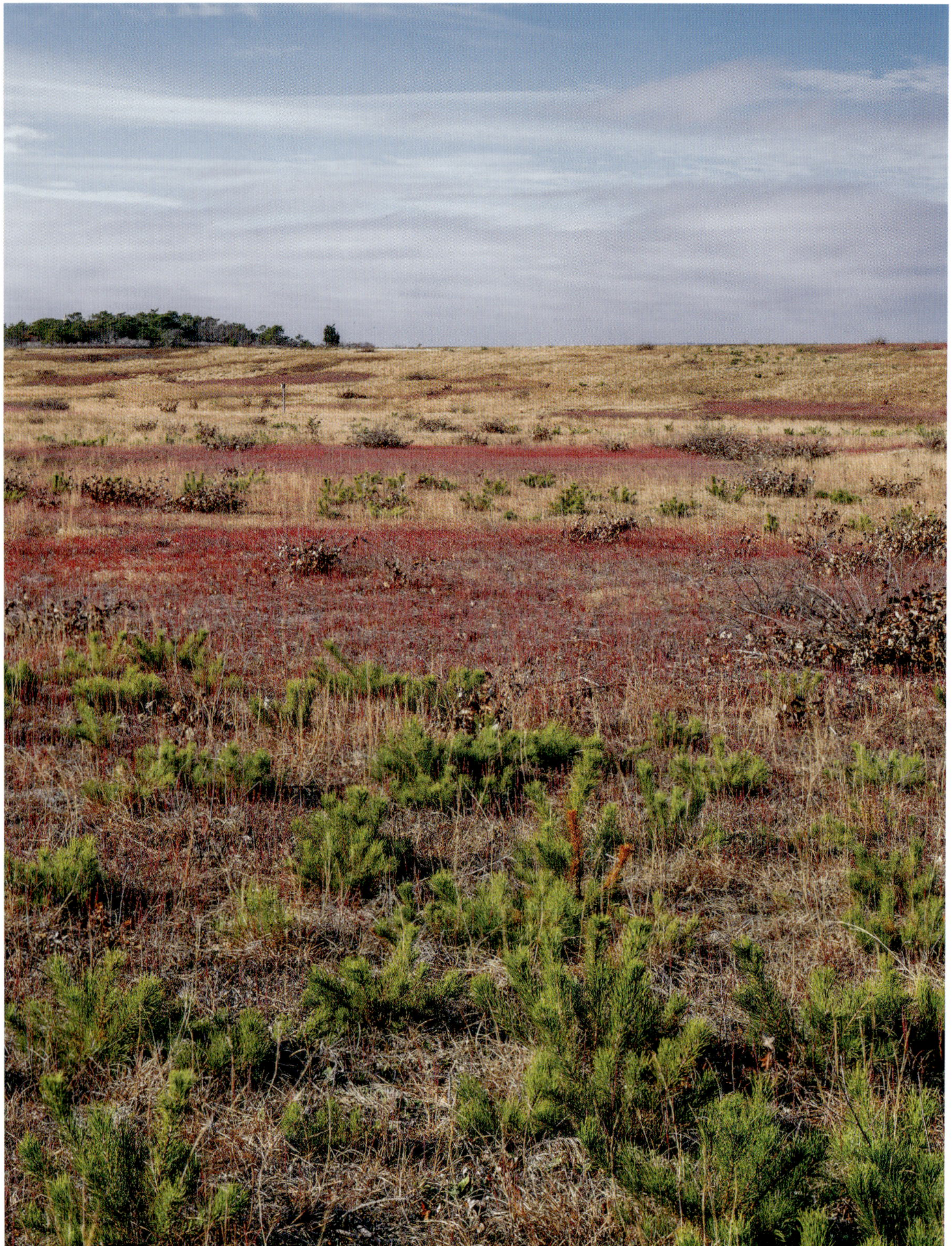

Bird House

Wasque Sand Plains, Chappaquiddick

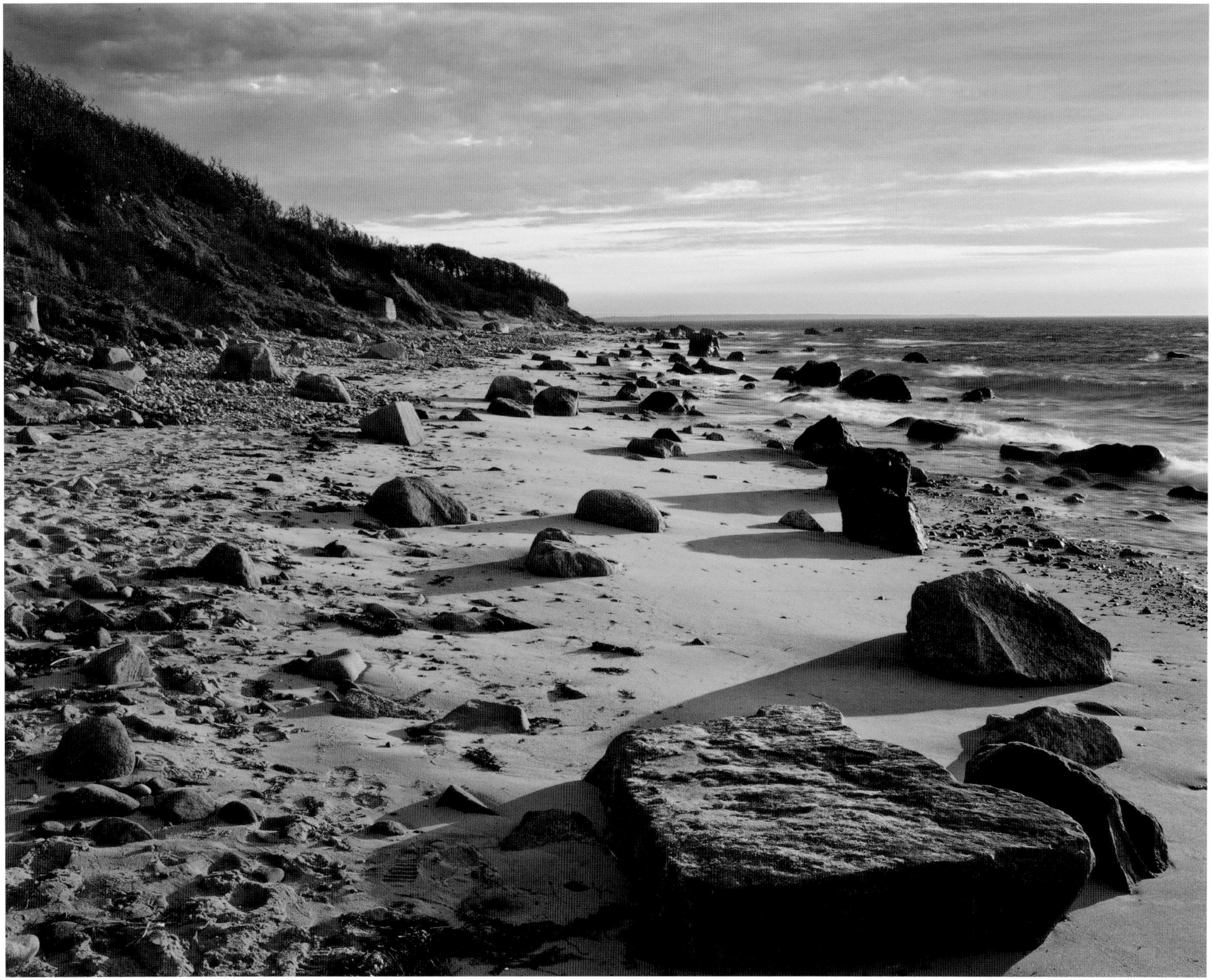

Late Light

Cedar Tree Neck, West Tisbury

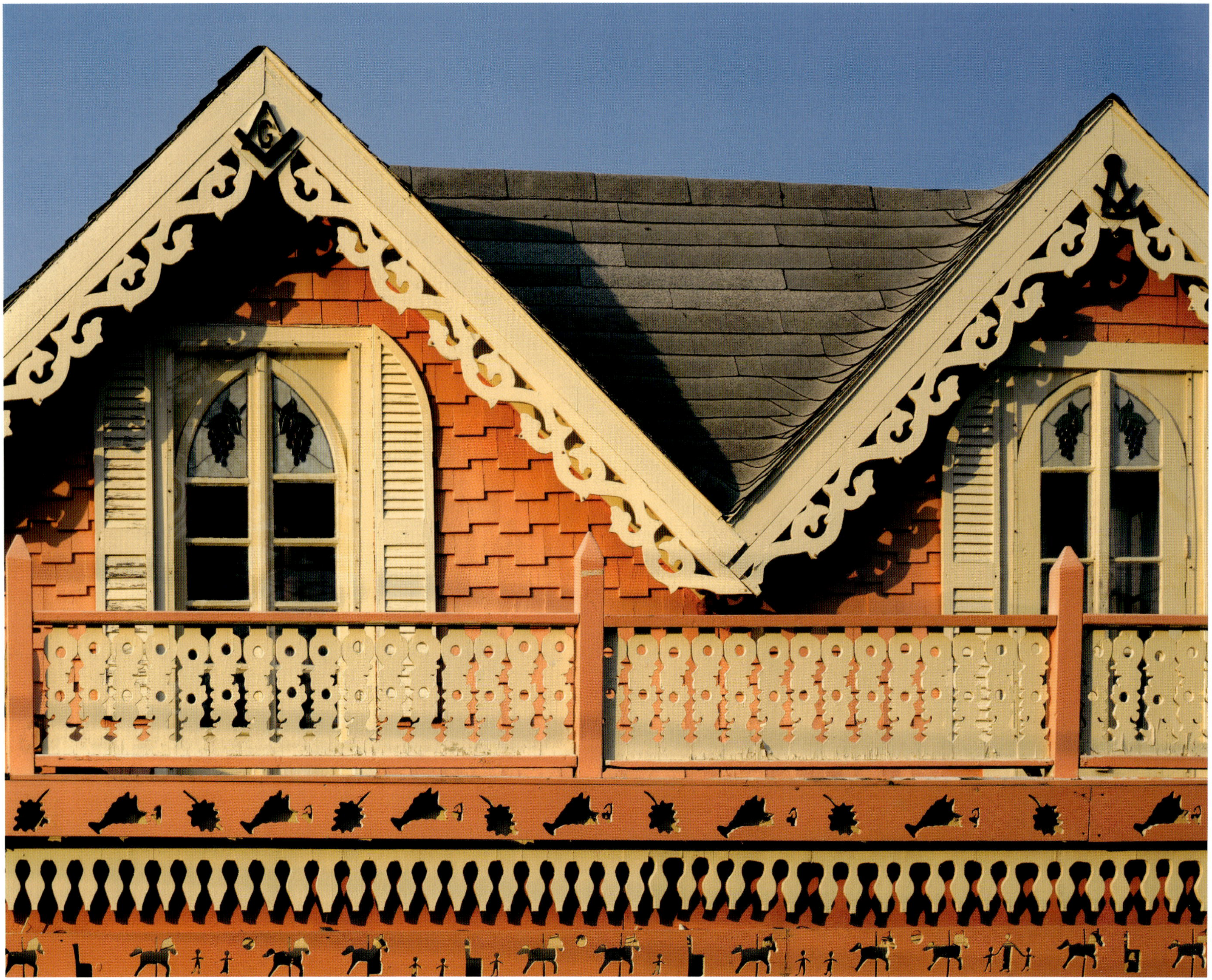

Wild Wood

Oak Bluffs

✦SPRING✦

THE LAST SNOWS HAVE MELTED. THE CROCUSES AND daffodils poked their green heads out of the thawing ground weeks ago. The screech owls can be heard. Who will hear the first "pinkle-tinks" or peepers, the tiny noisy tree frogs (*Hyla crucifer*) whose high-pitched mating calls are the starting whistle of spring on the Vineyard? The migratory flight paths fill up overhead as the Vineyard plays host to thousands of birds heading back to their summer digs, both here and farther north. The ospreys return. Terns make their first bold seasonal dives, miniature bombers swooping low over the water as the piping plovers begin to nest nearby.

Landscapers, electricians, plumbers, carpenters, and painters work overtime to finish their projects before the migration of summer people begins. Houses and shops get new coats of paint. The Steamship Authority boats, the ferries that are the Island's lifeline, are serviced and cleaned. Moorings are checked and the harbors begin to fill with sloops, yawls, and ketches, bright work varnished, awaiting their crews. Shop shelves are stocked, though their doors remain locked. Each week a few more restaurants end their hibernation. Summerhouses are aired out, gutters cleaned, and the water is turned on. The tapes are laid and nets are strung on the island's many tennis courts. Spring at last.

—*T.O.*

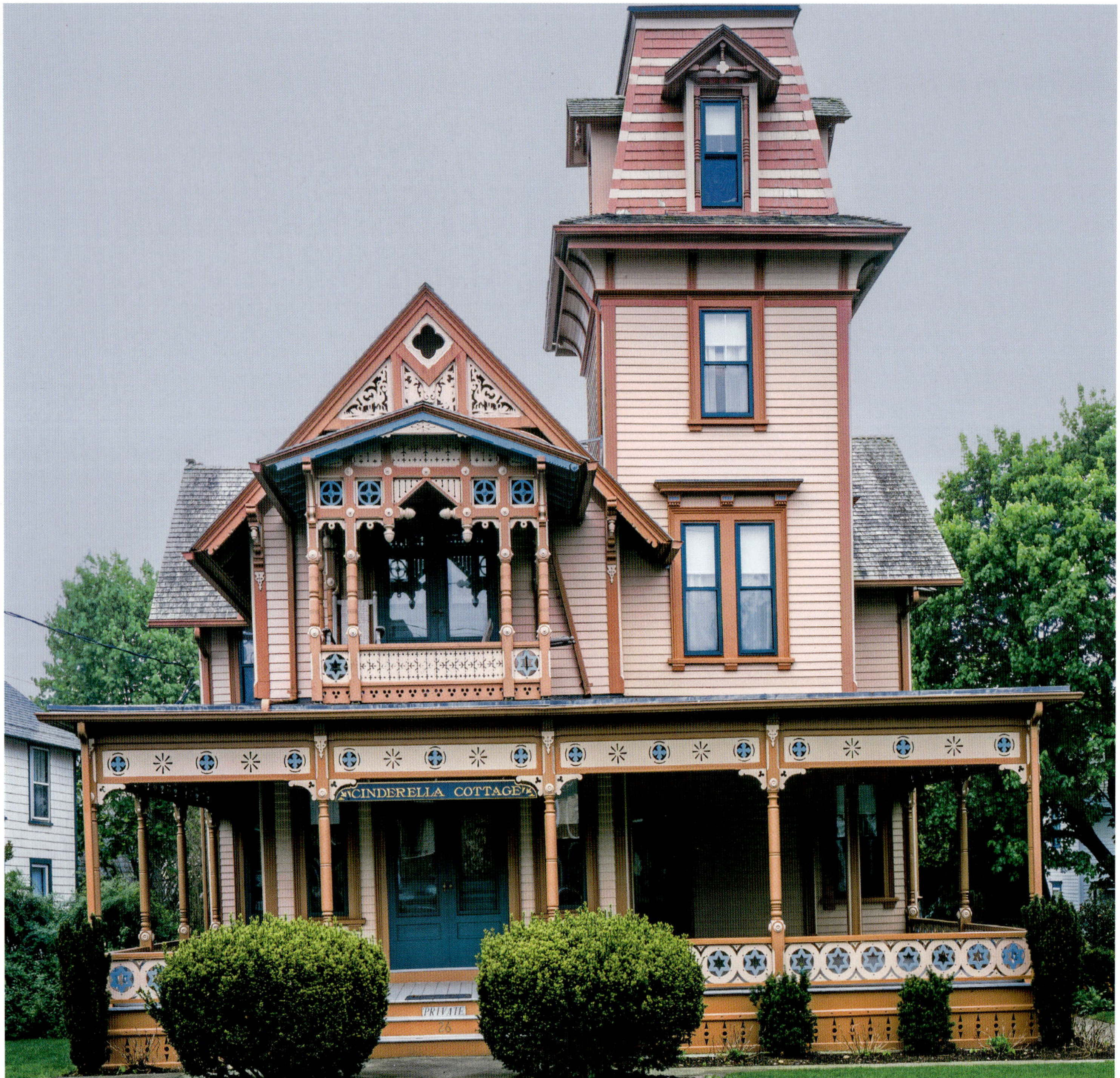

Cinderella Cottage Oak Bluffs

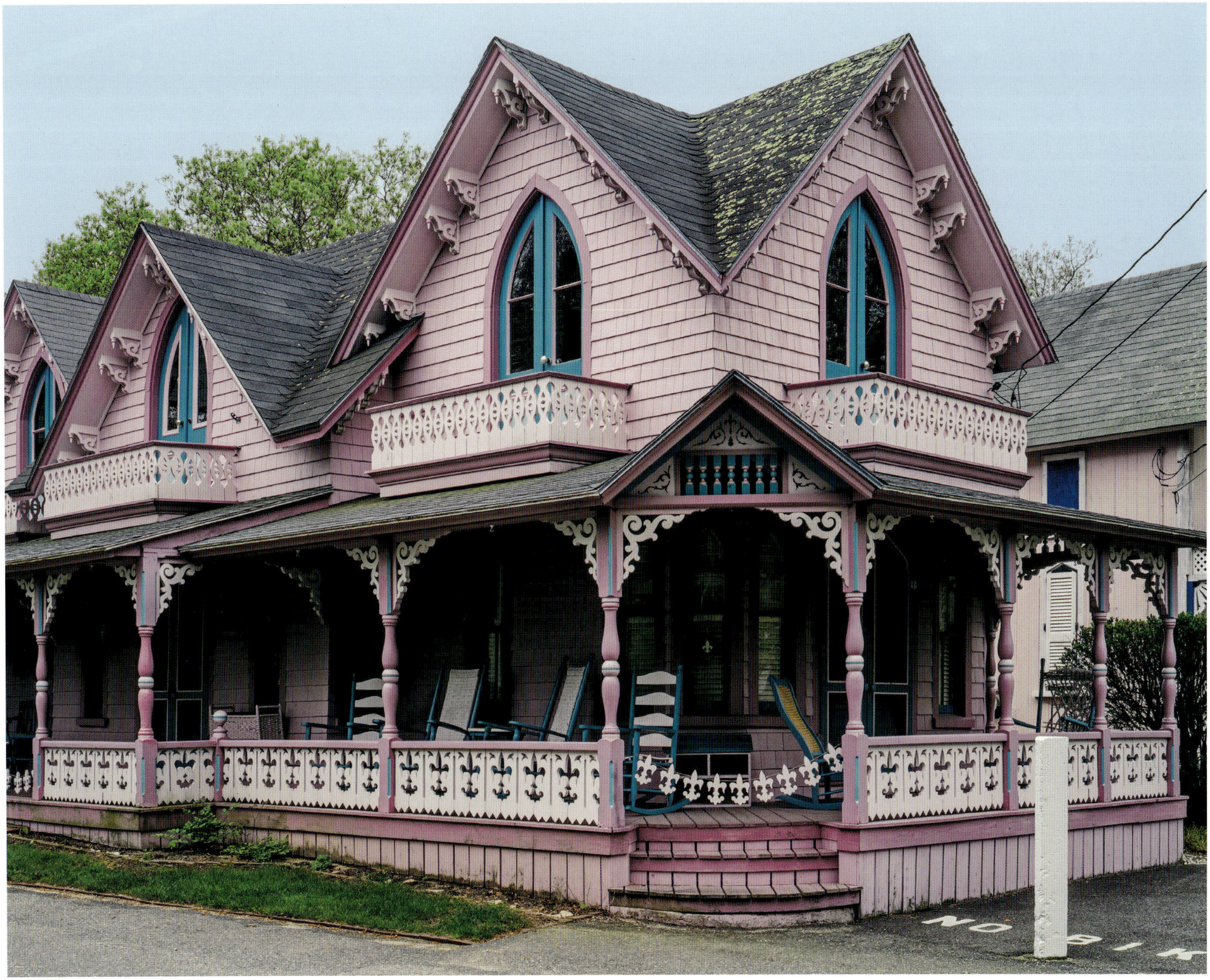

Fleur de Lis

Oak Bluffs

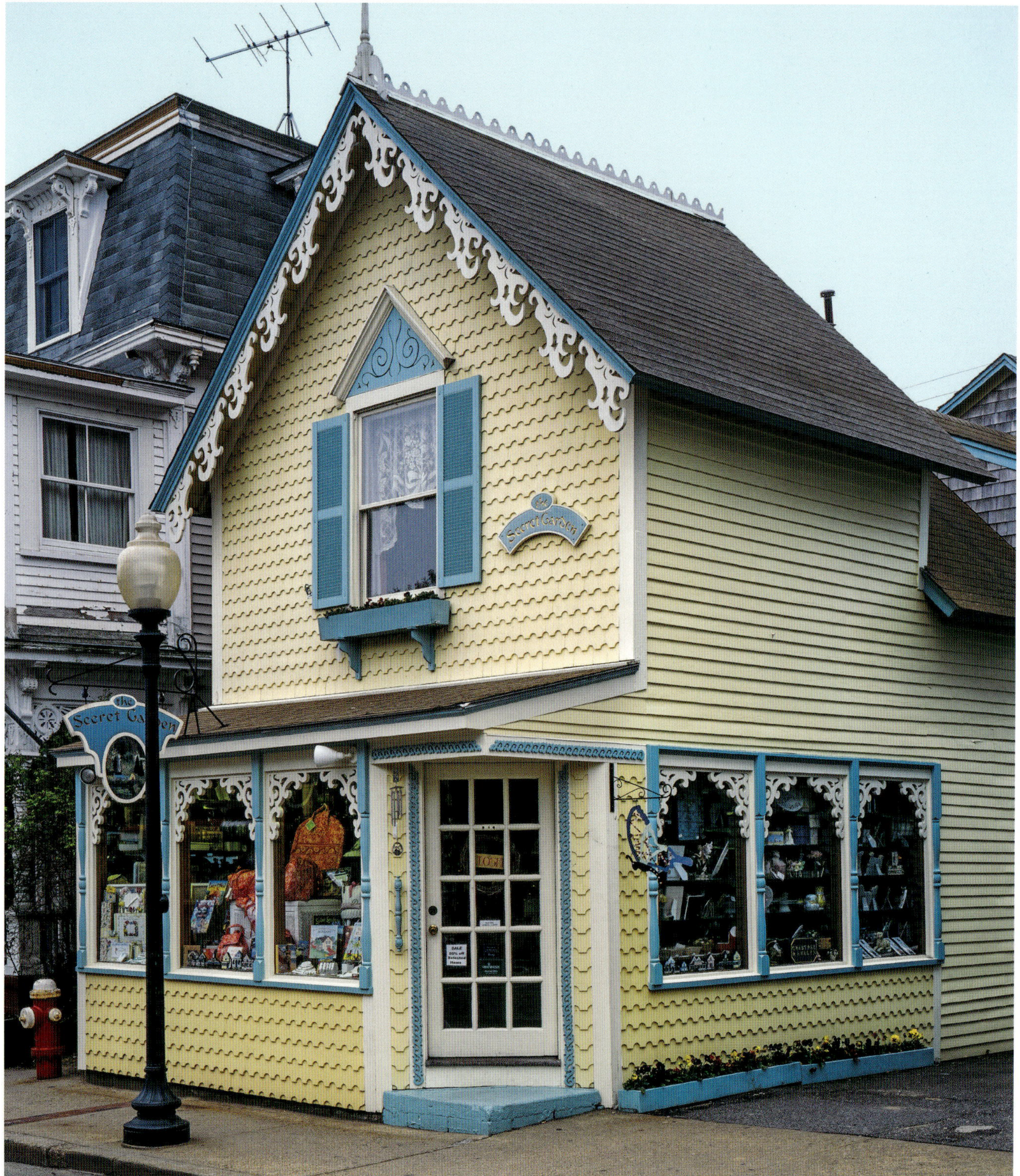

Secret Garden

Oak Bluffs

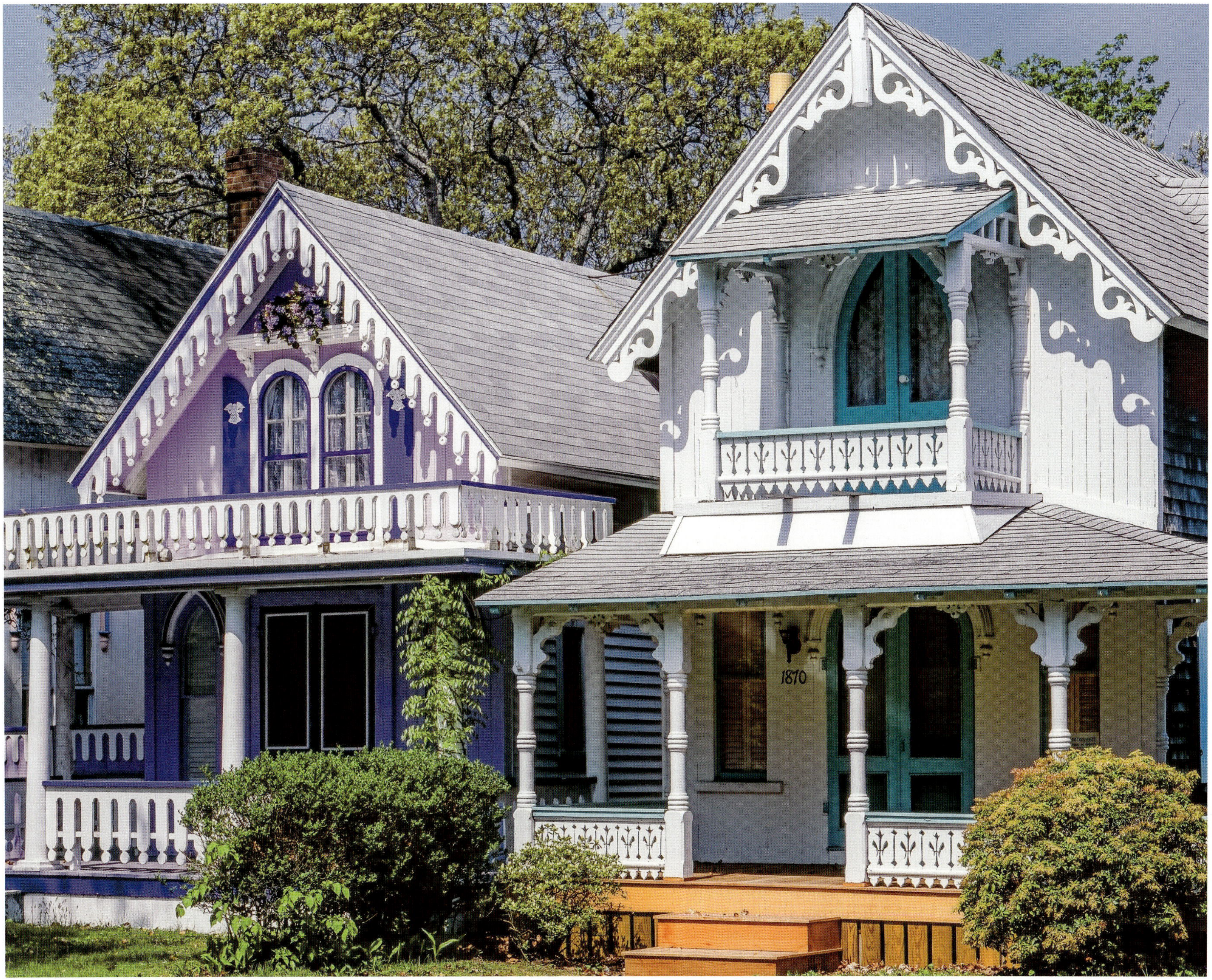

Gingerbread Couple Oak Bluffs

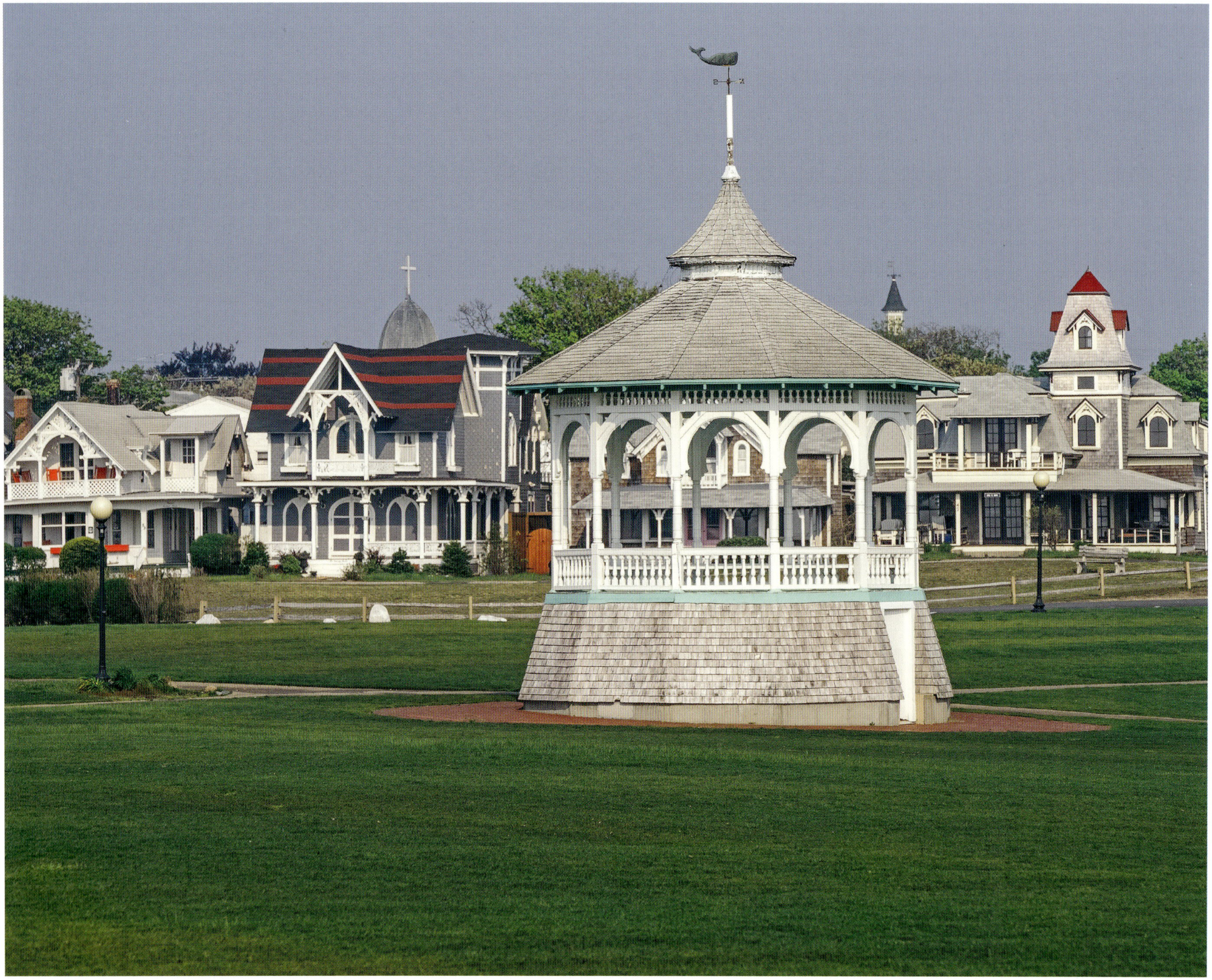

Ocean Park Gazebo

Oak Bluffs

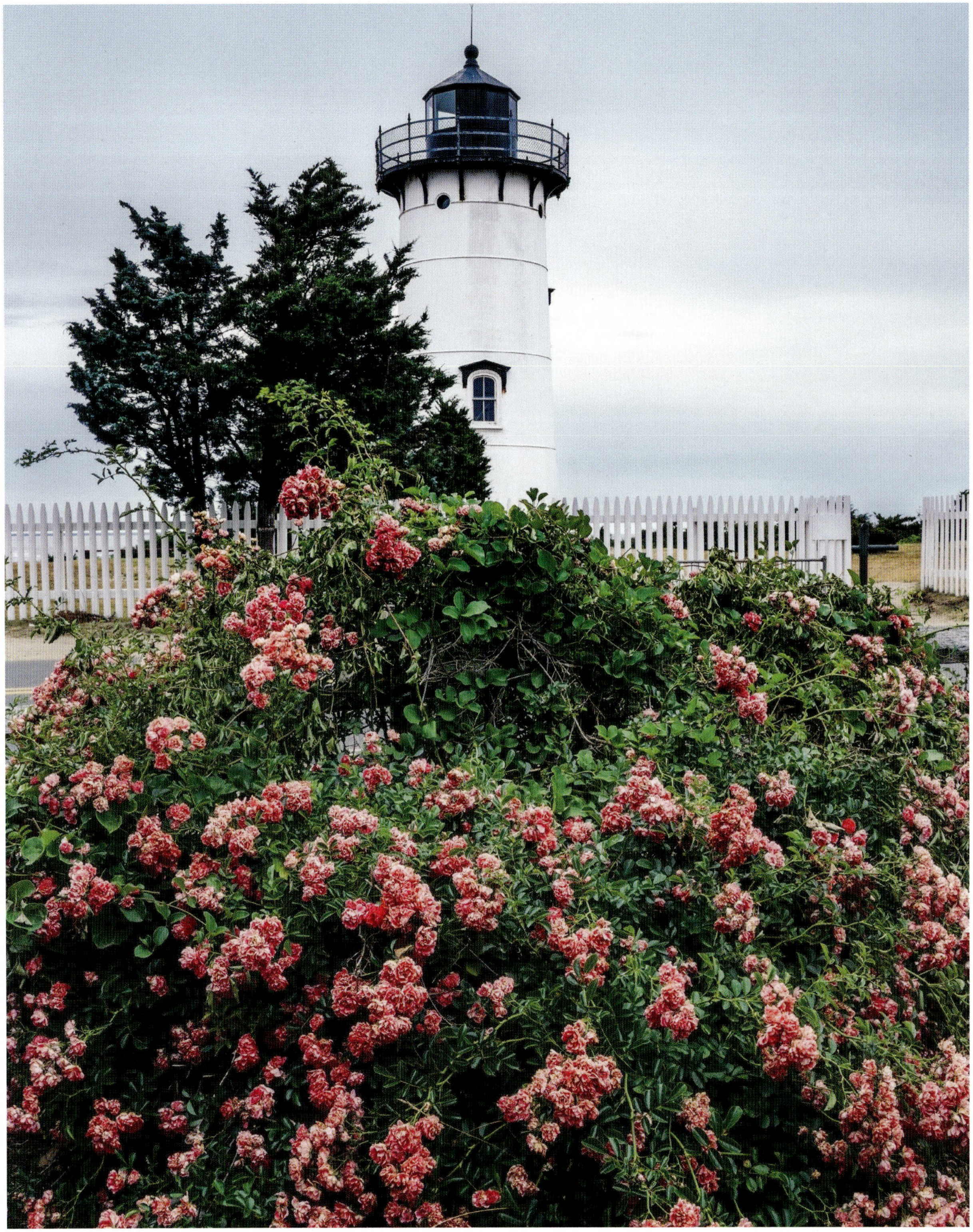

Wild Roses

East Chop Lighthouse, Oak Bluffs

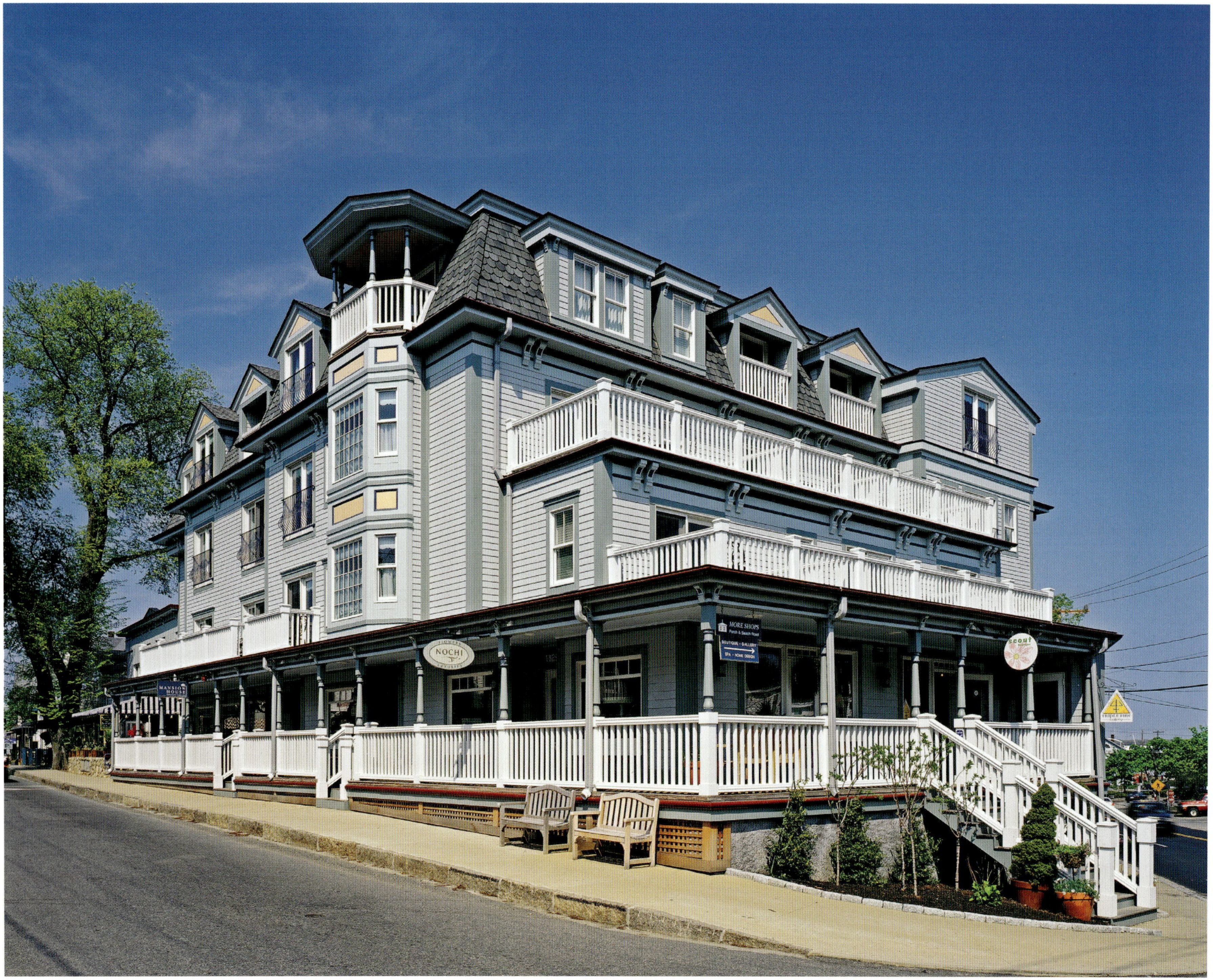

Mansion House

Vineyard Haven

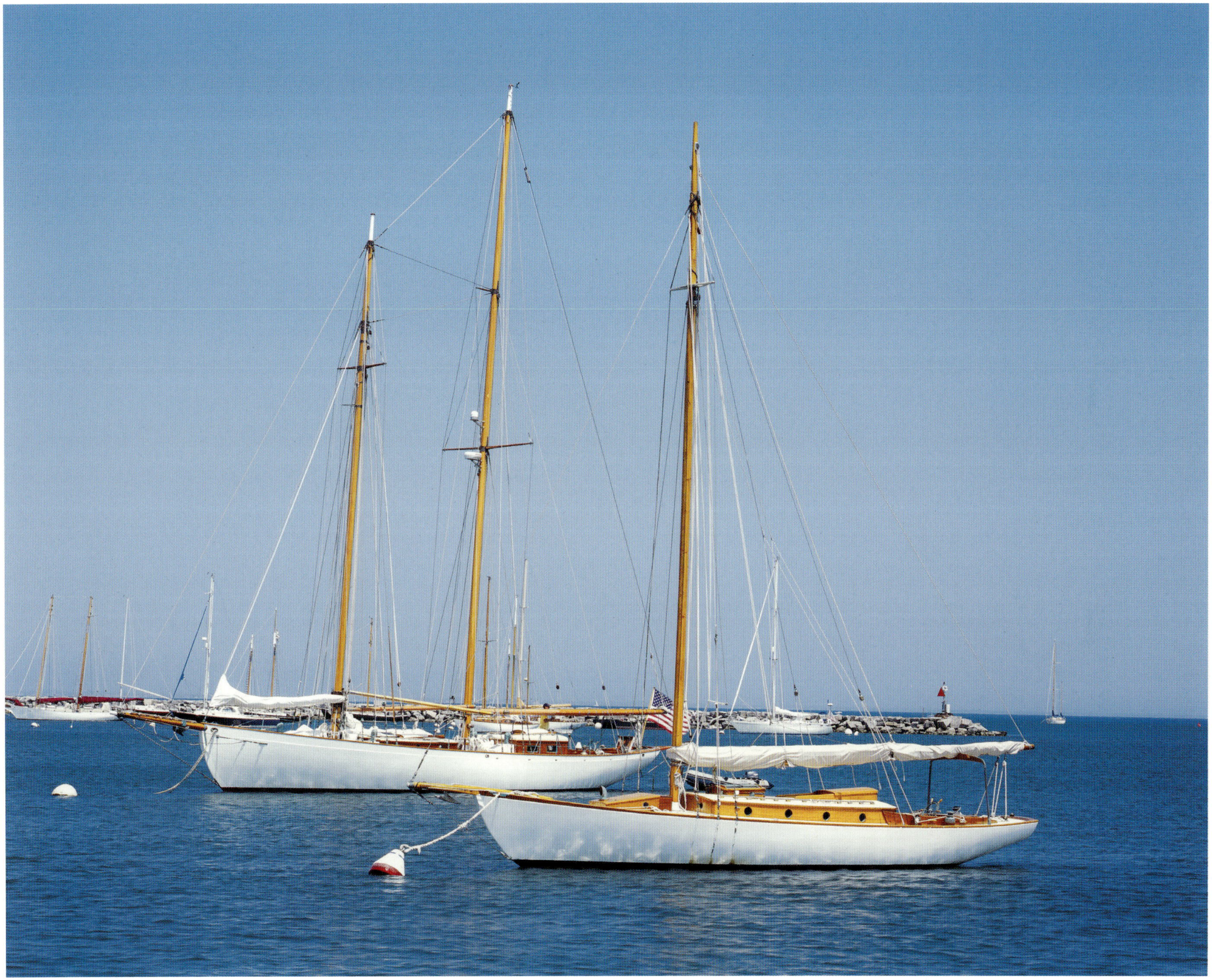

Wooden Boats

Vineyard Haven Harbor

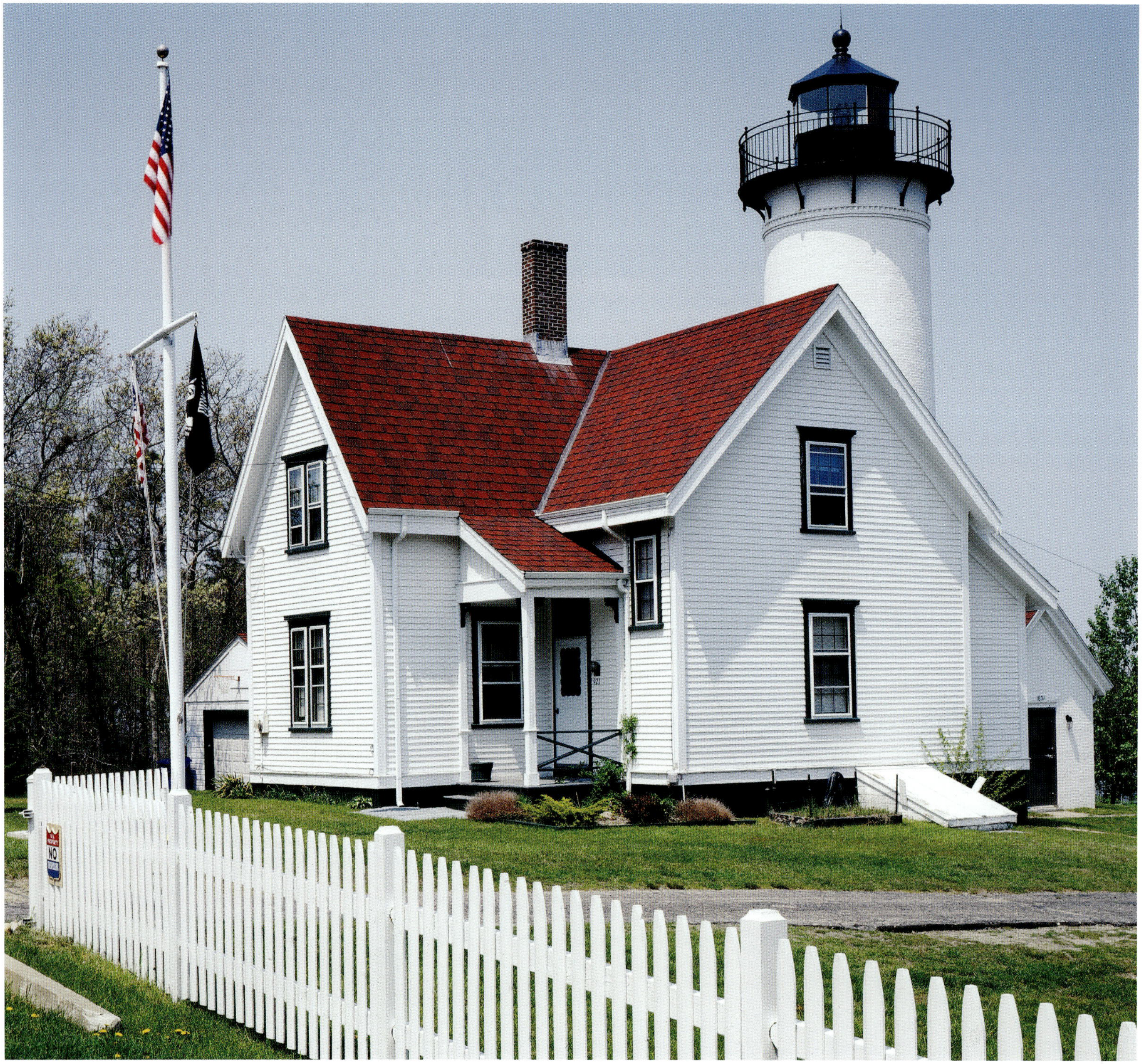

West Chop Lighthouse

Tisbury

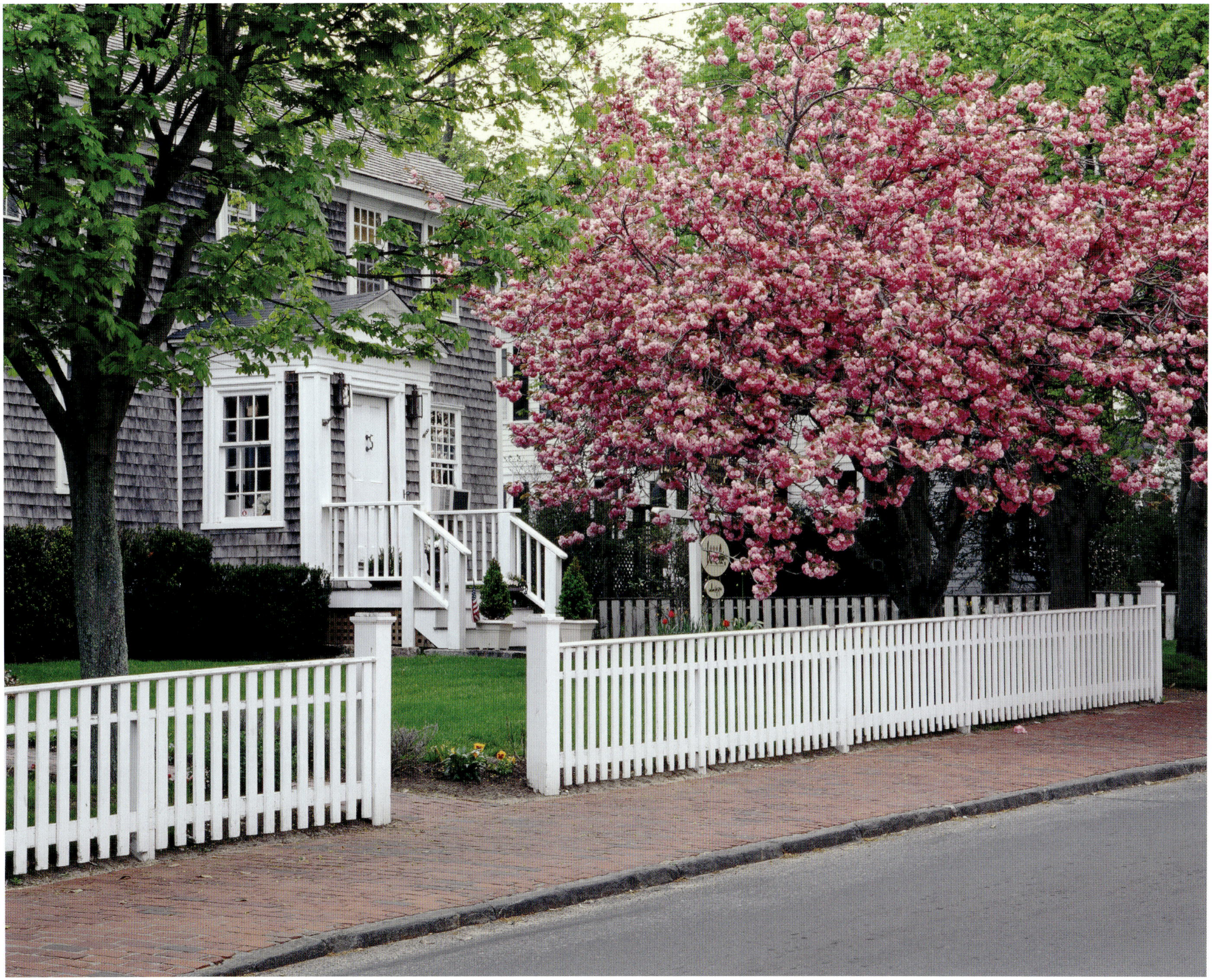

In Bloom

Edgartown

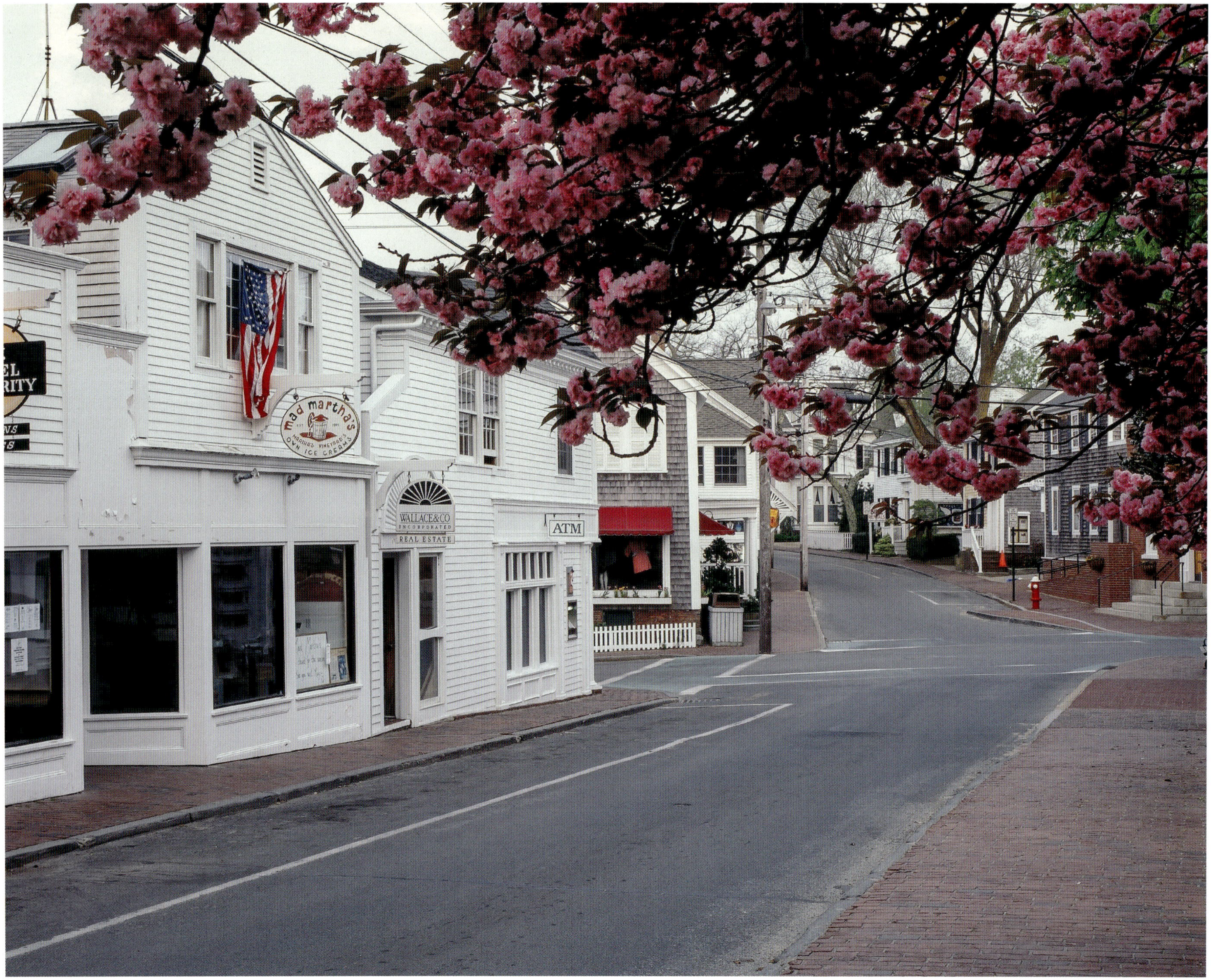

North Water St. Edgartown

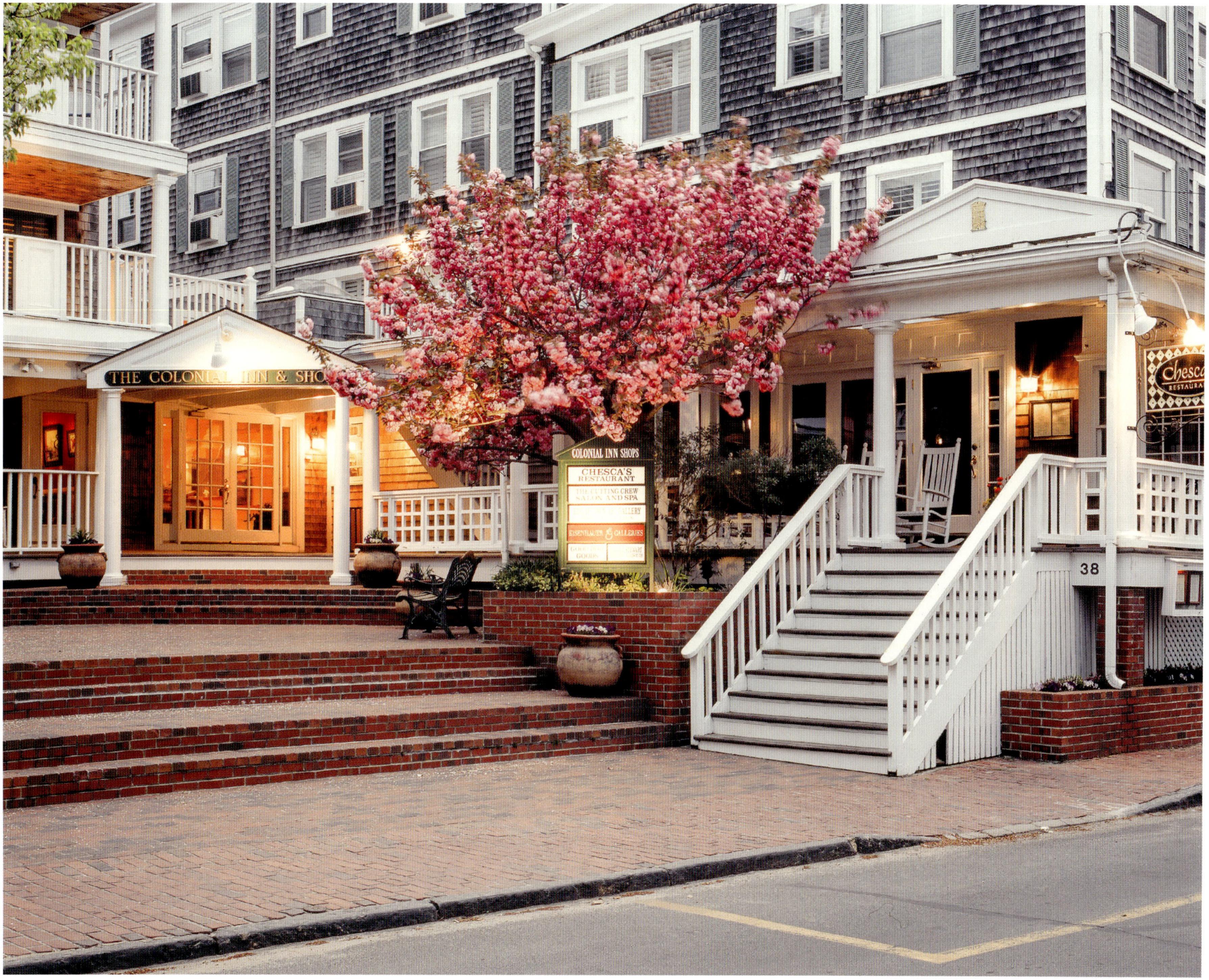

North Main St. Edgartown

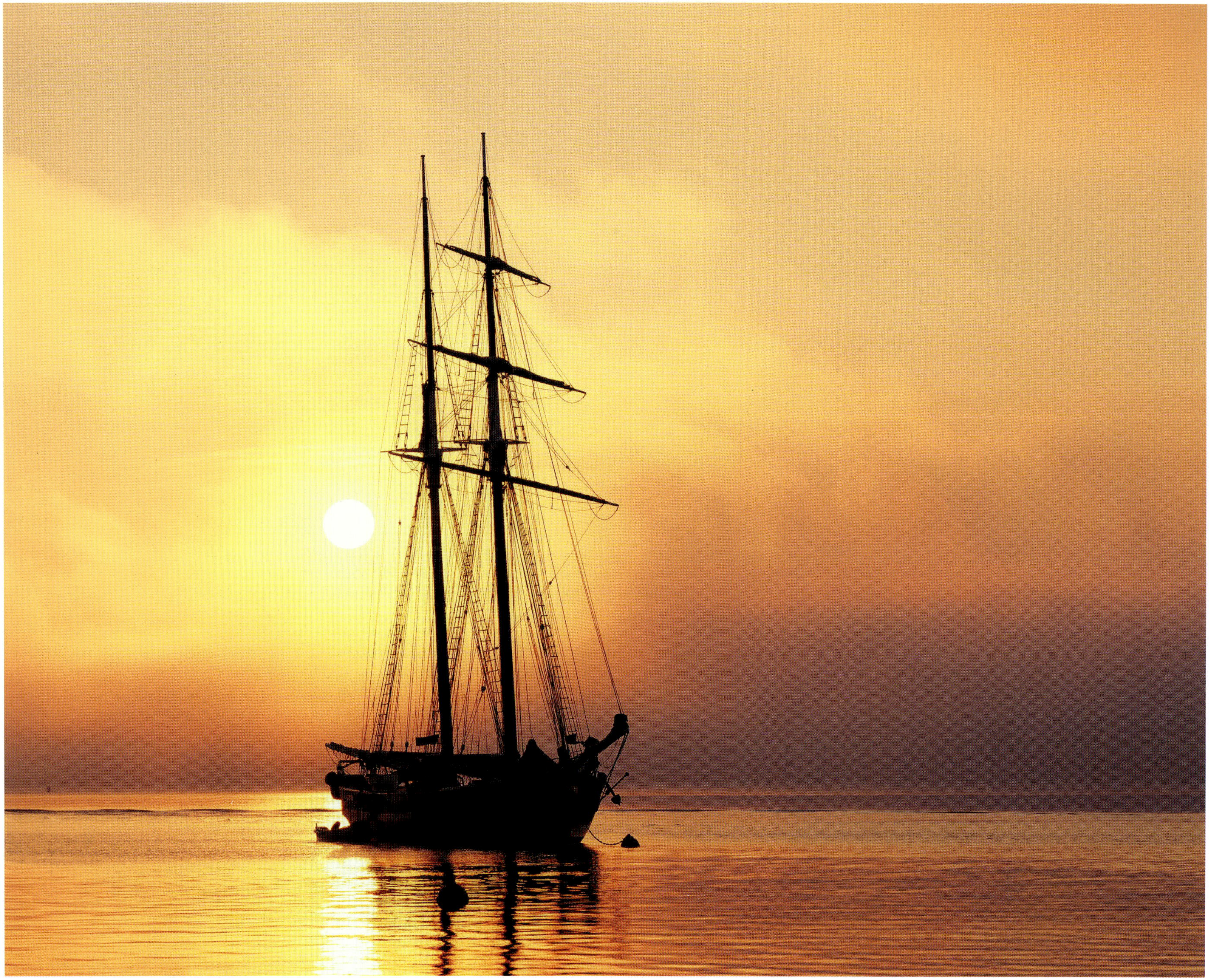

Shenandoah at Sunrise

Vineyard Haven Harbor

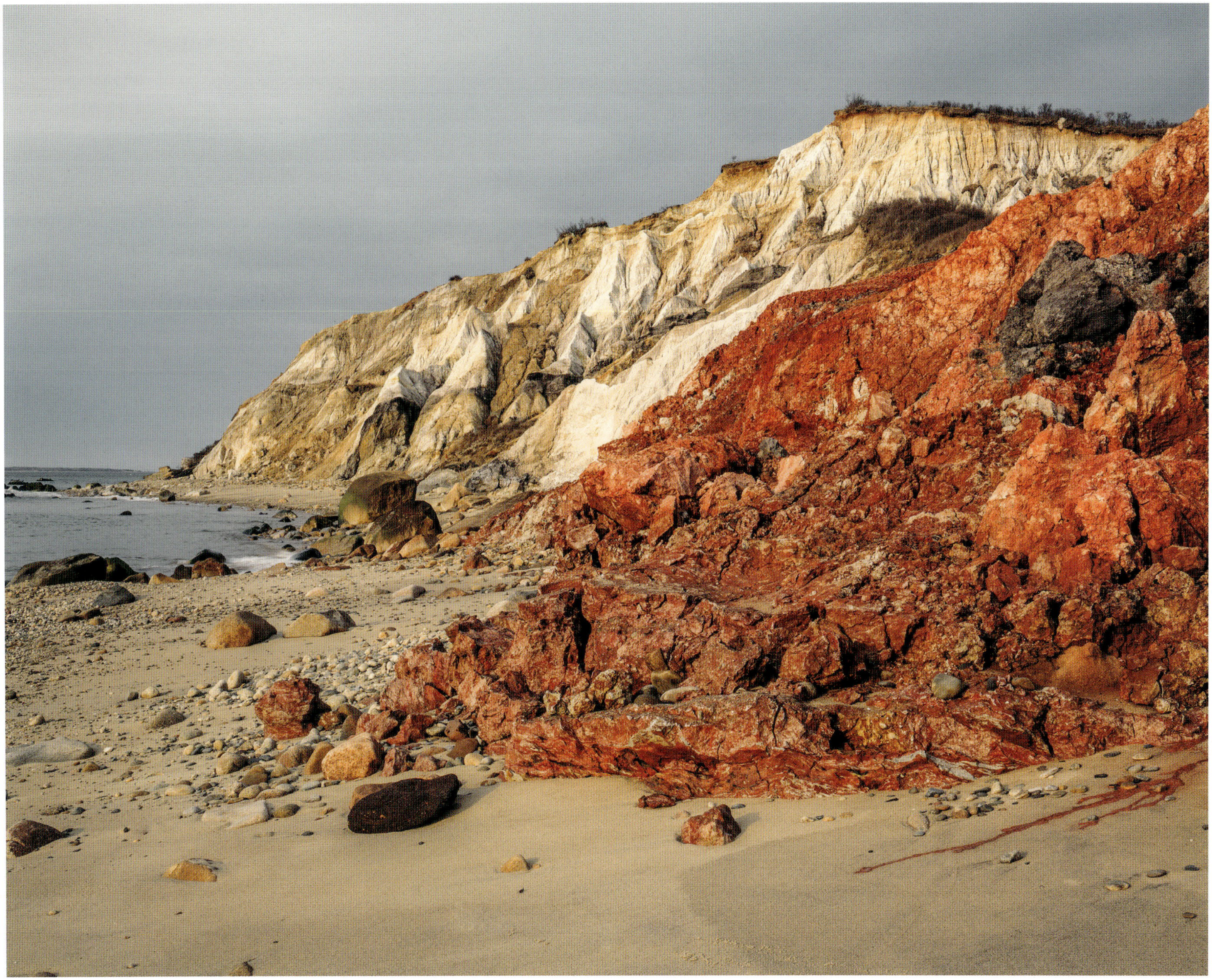

Running Red

Gay Head Cliffs, Aquinnah

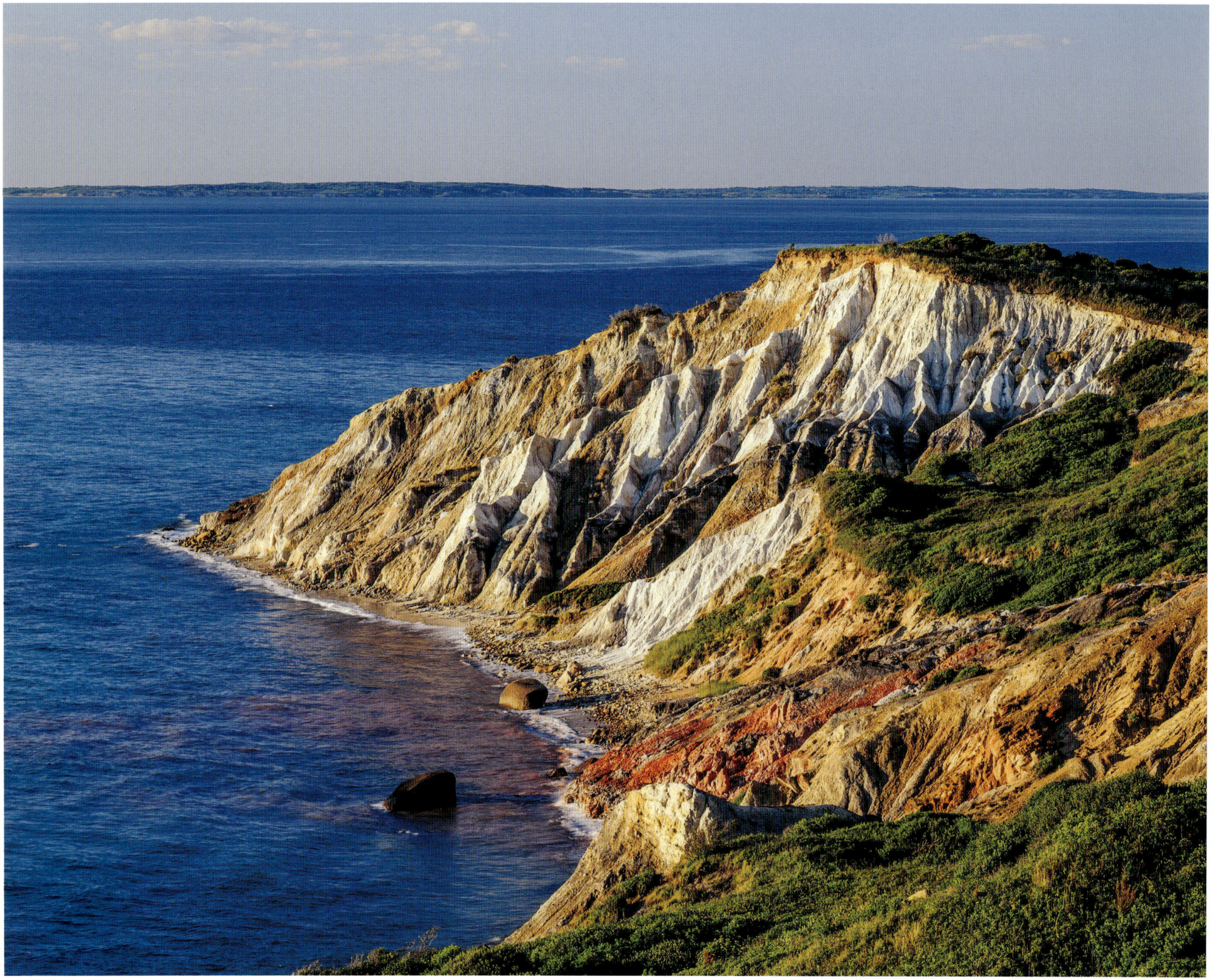

Gay Head

Aquinnah

✦SUMMER✦

WHAT BRINGS VISITORS BACK TO THE VINEYARD year after year? What is it about the Vineyard that attracts families for a week or two, or a month, or even permanently? It's usually the summer, the Vineyard's full-tilt boogie. Escape the city heat. Hit the beaches. There are sandcastles waiting to be built, and shells to be collected. Hank on the sails. Check the lines. Renew the fishing tackle. Fish are waiting, so are the scallops and clams. Don't forget the kayak or canoe. The golf courses are groomed and green. The tennis clubs are open. The woodland trails are calling. Bring your bikes and hiking shoes. There's no big-city traffic here, not even a stoplight. And the bike paths and hiking trails go almost everywhere. Restaurants, real night-life, ice cream, and fudge beckon. Don't forget to bring home a T-shirt. Where's the camera?

— *T.O.*

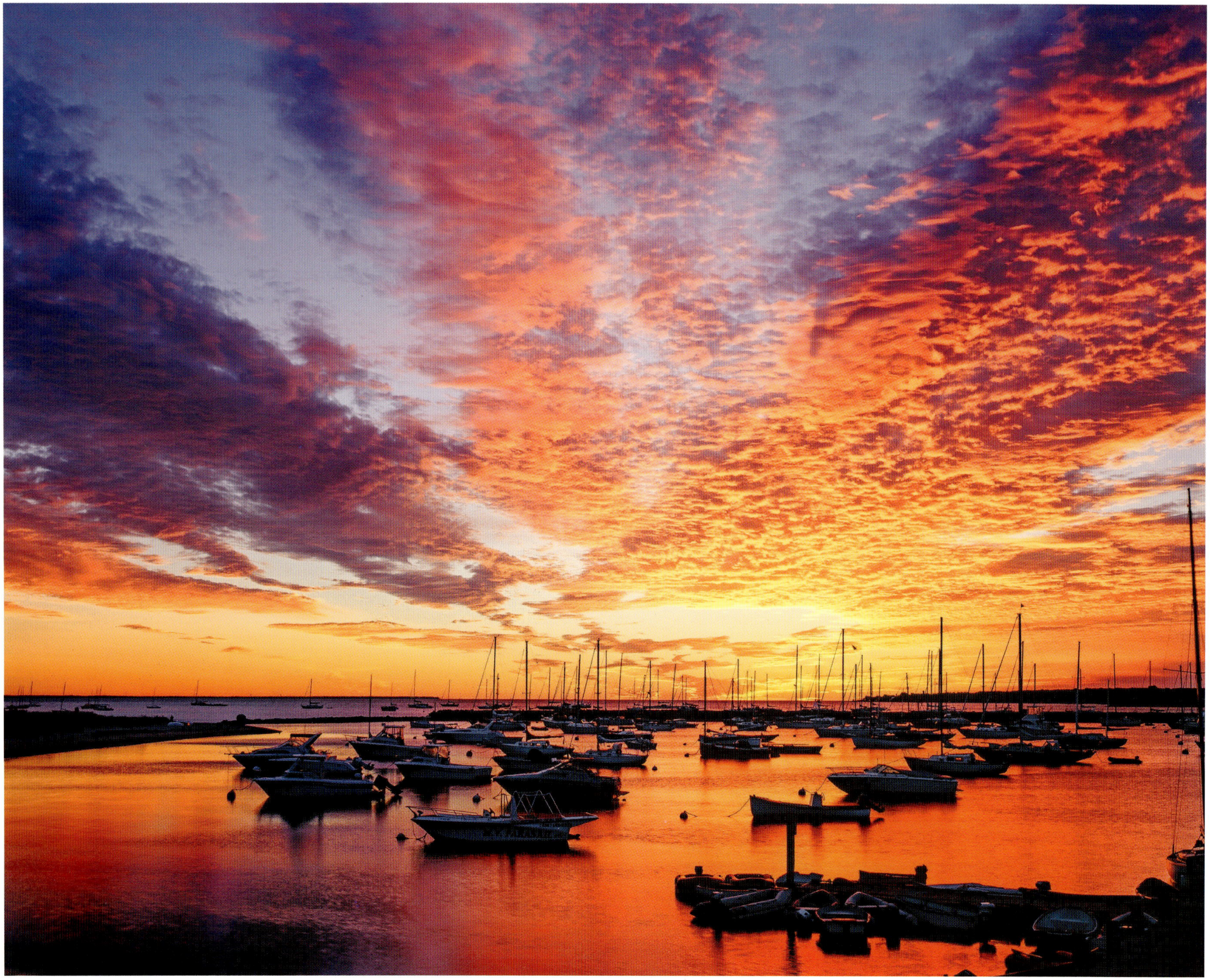

Uncertain Sunrise

Vineyard Haven Harbor

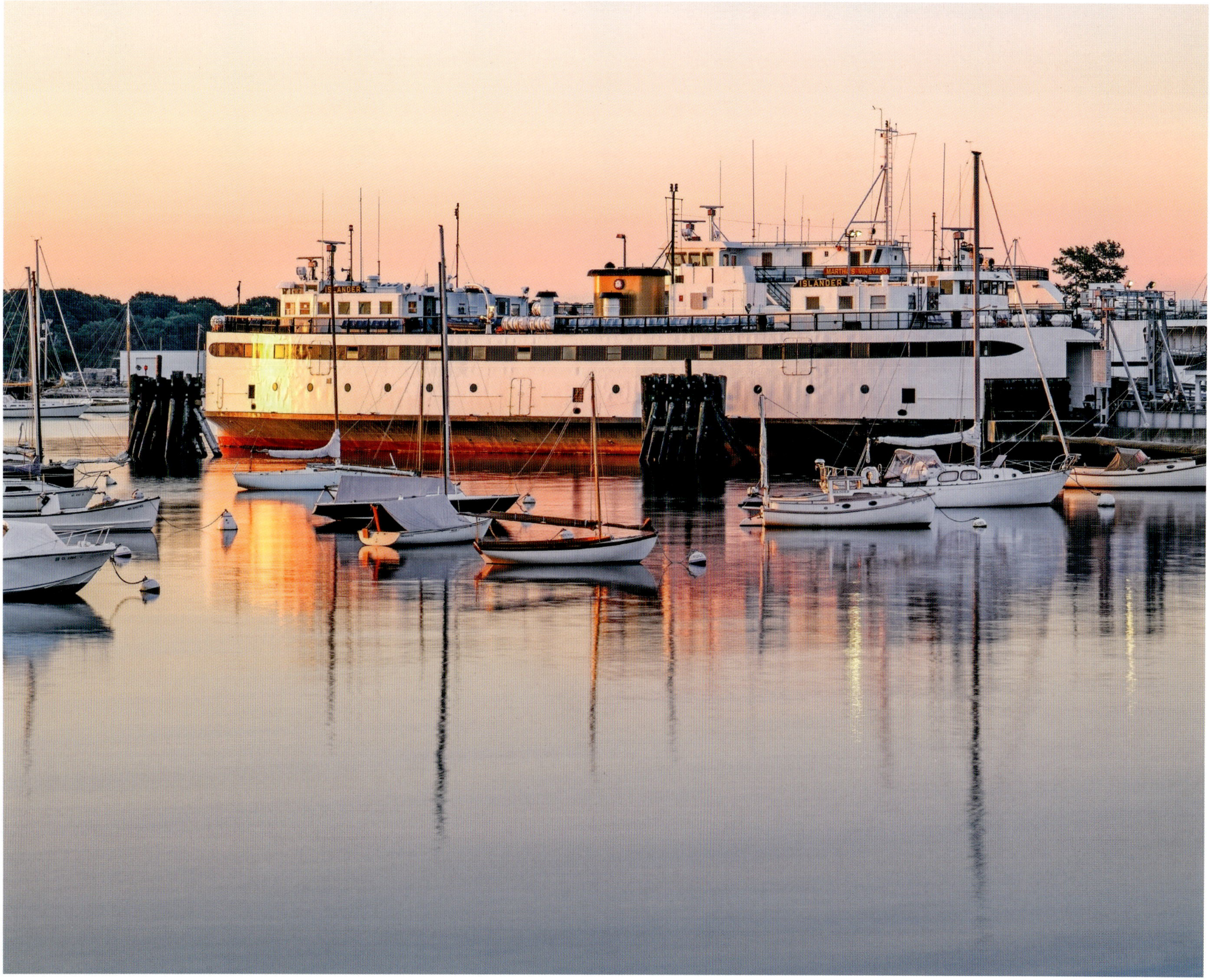

Islander

Vineyard Haven Harbor

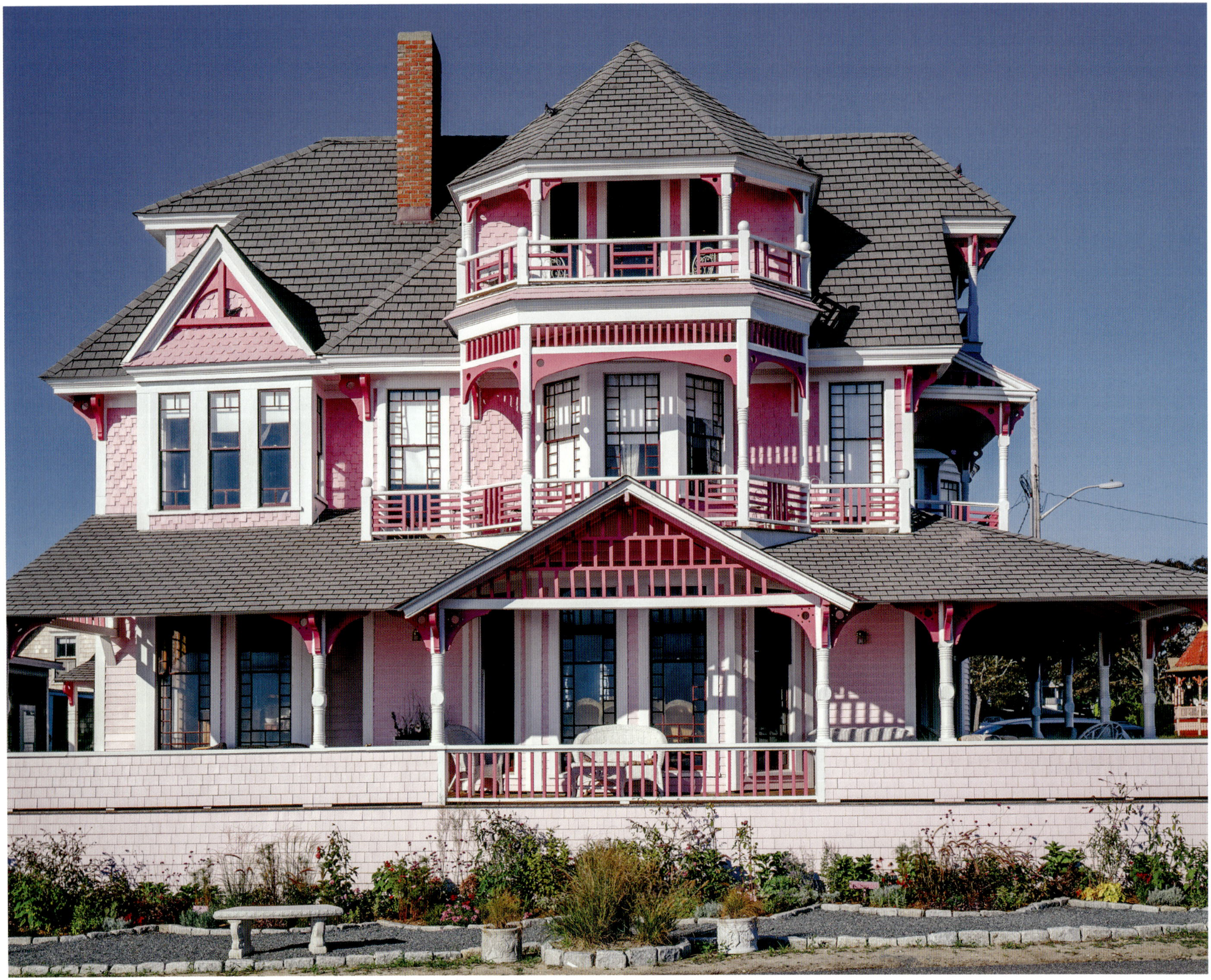

Gingerbread Rising

Oak Bluffs

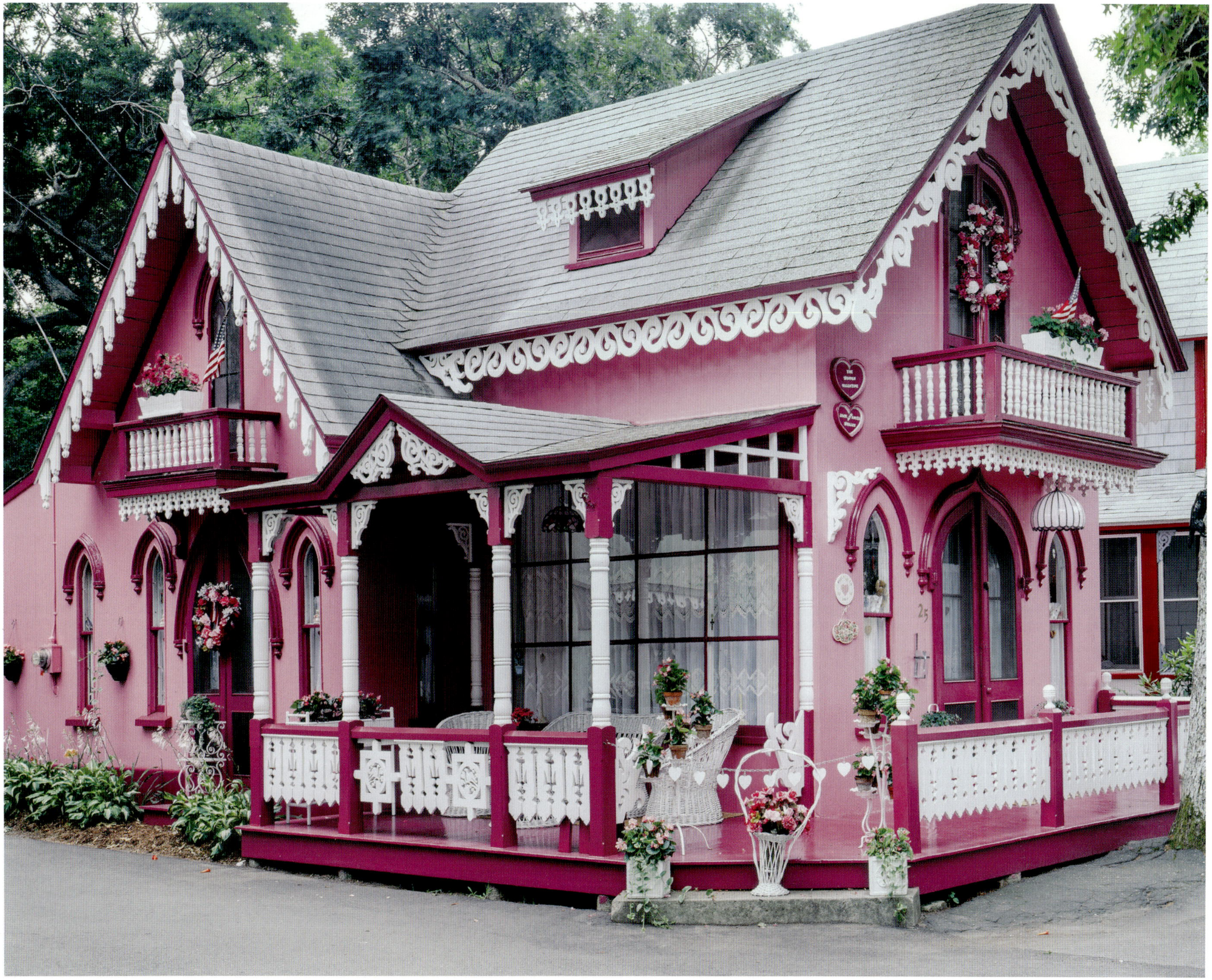

Rose House — Oak Bluffs

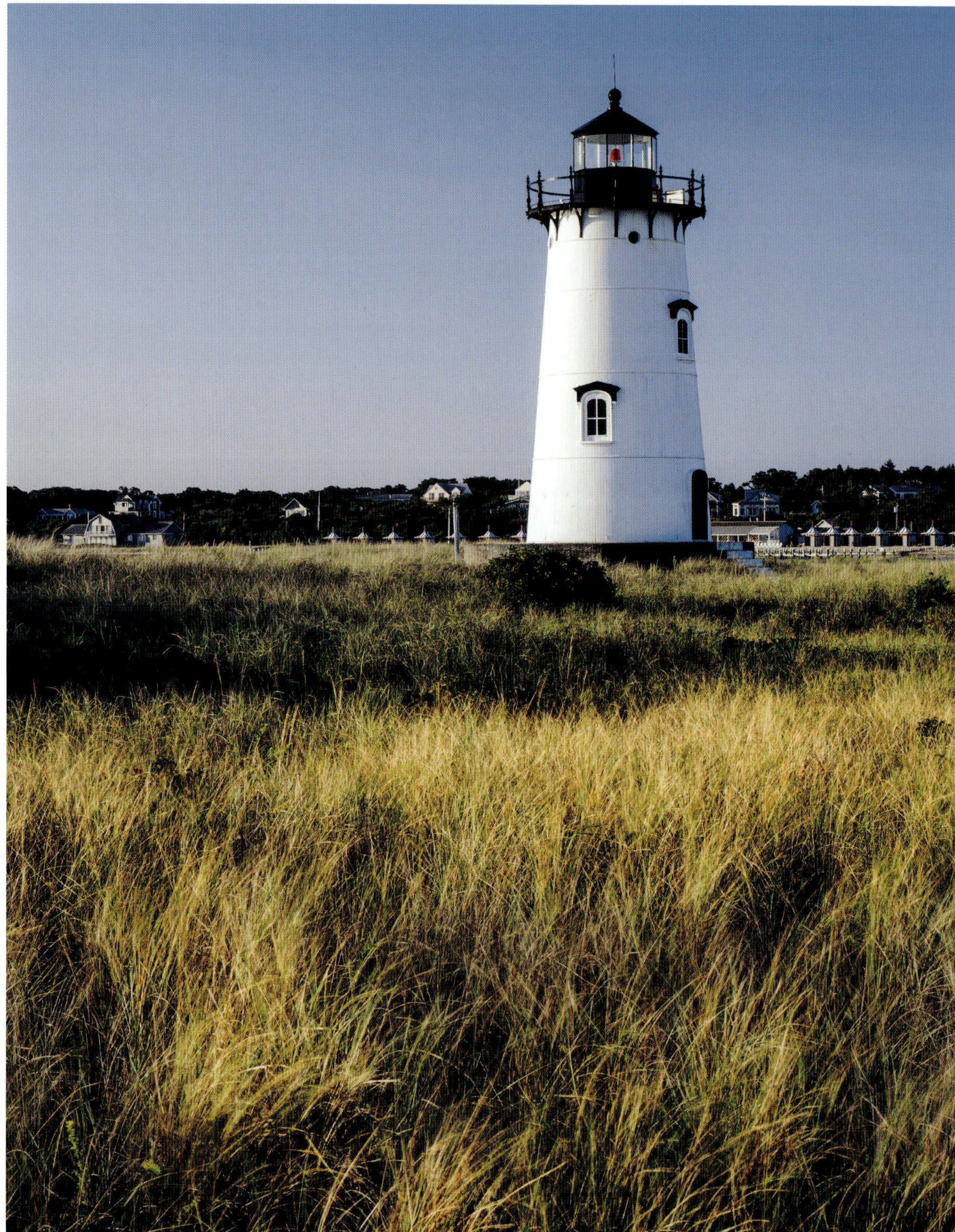

Beach Grass

Edgartown Lighthouse

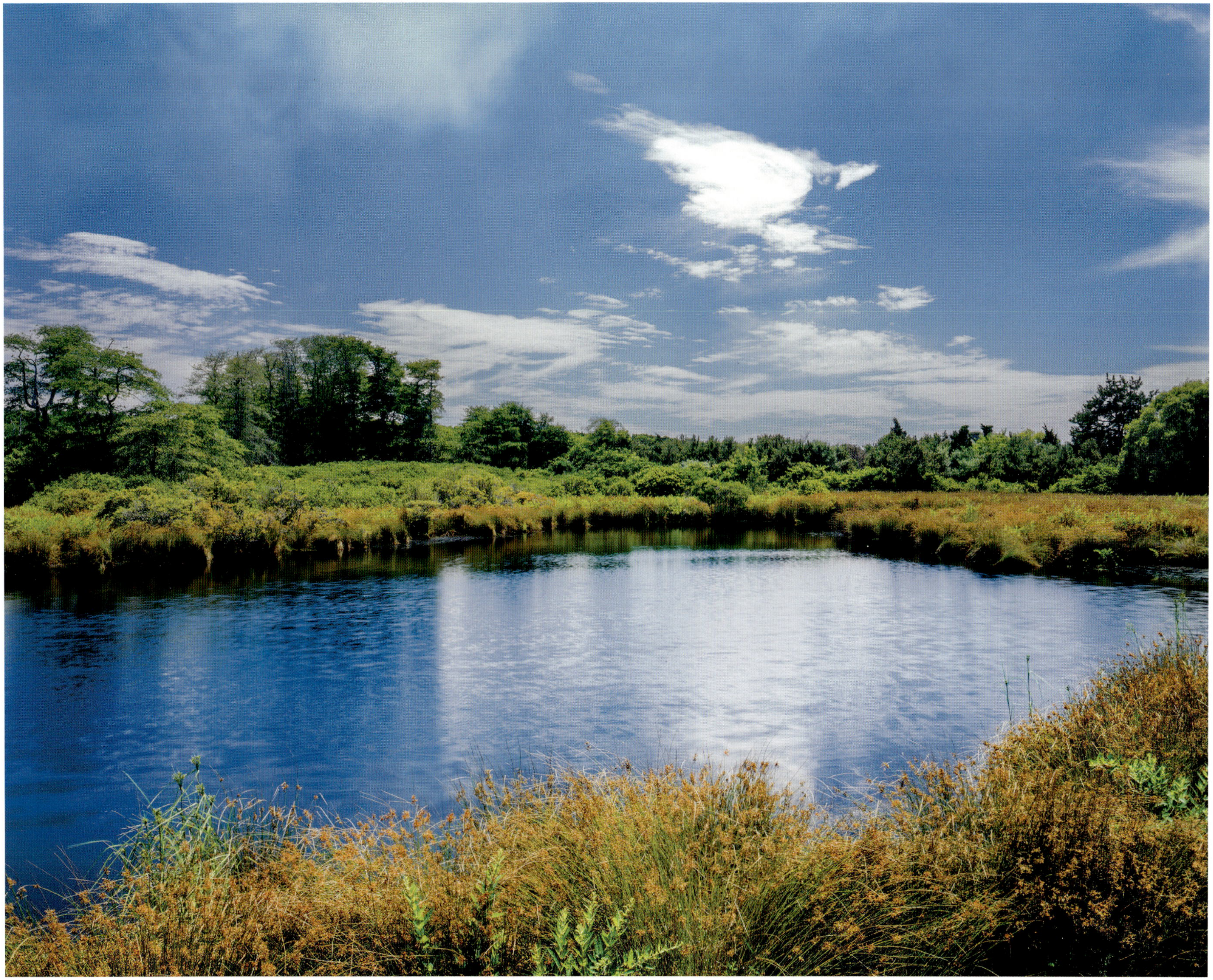

Summer Pond Edgartown

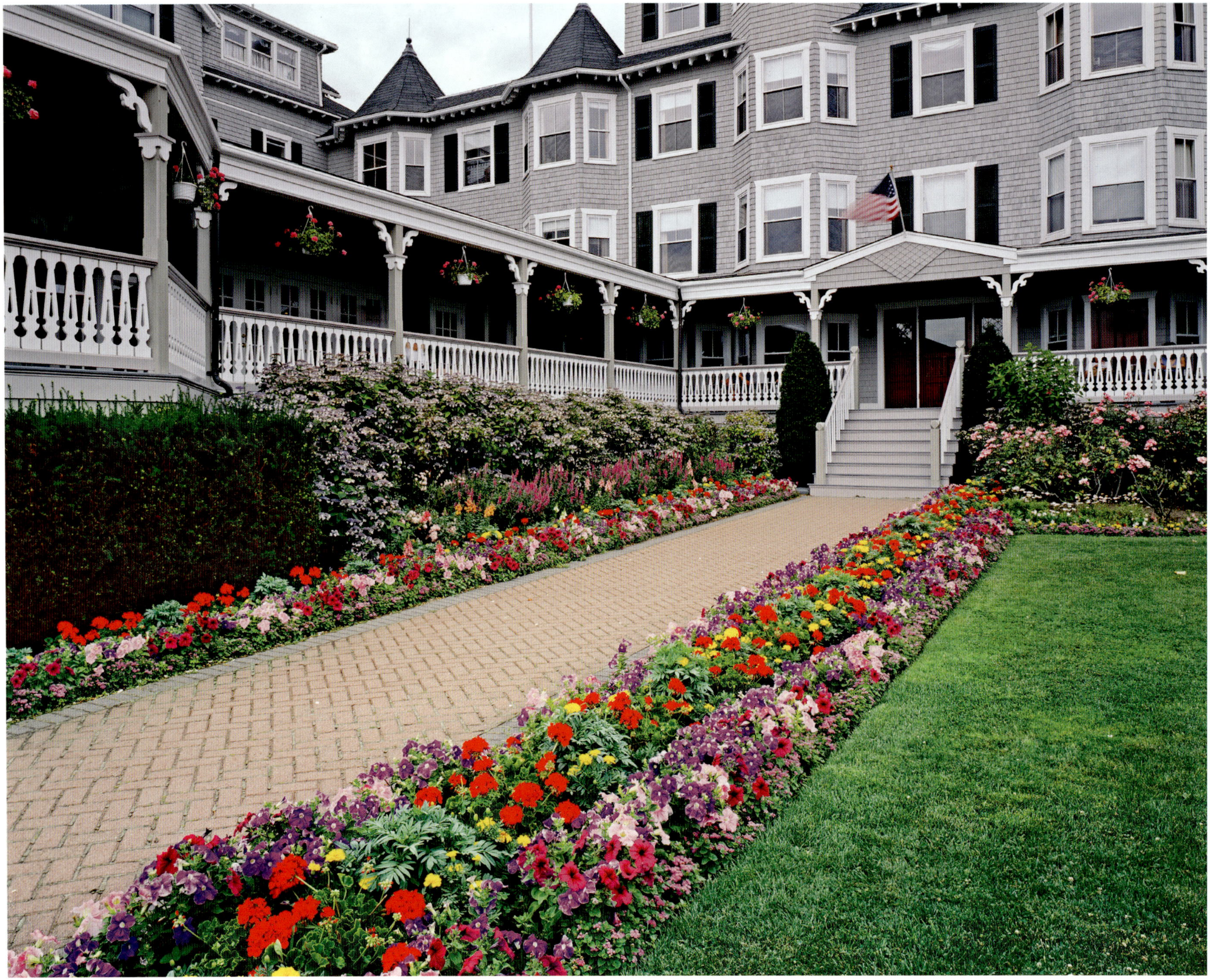

Harbor View Edgartown

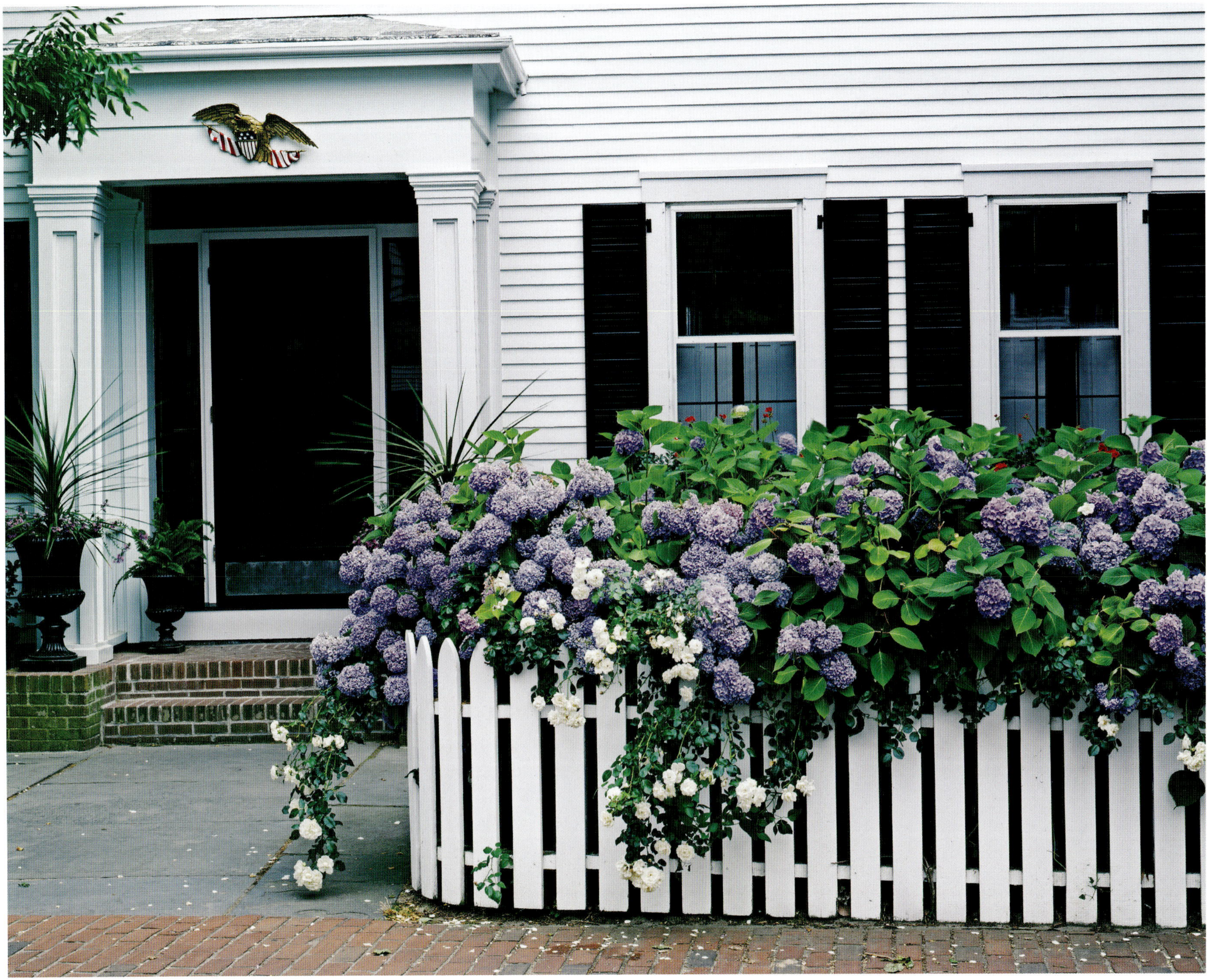

Purple Hydrangea Edgartown

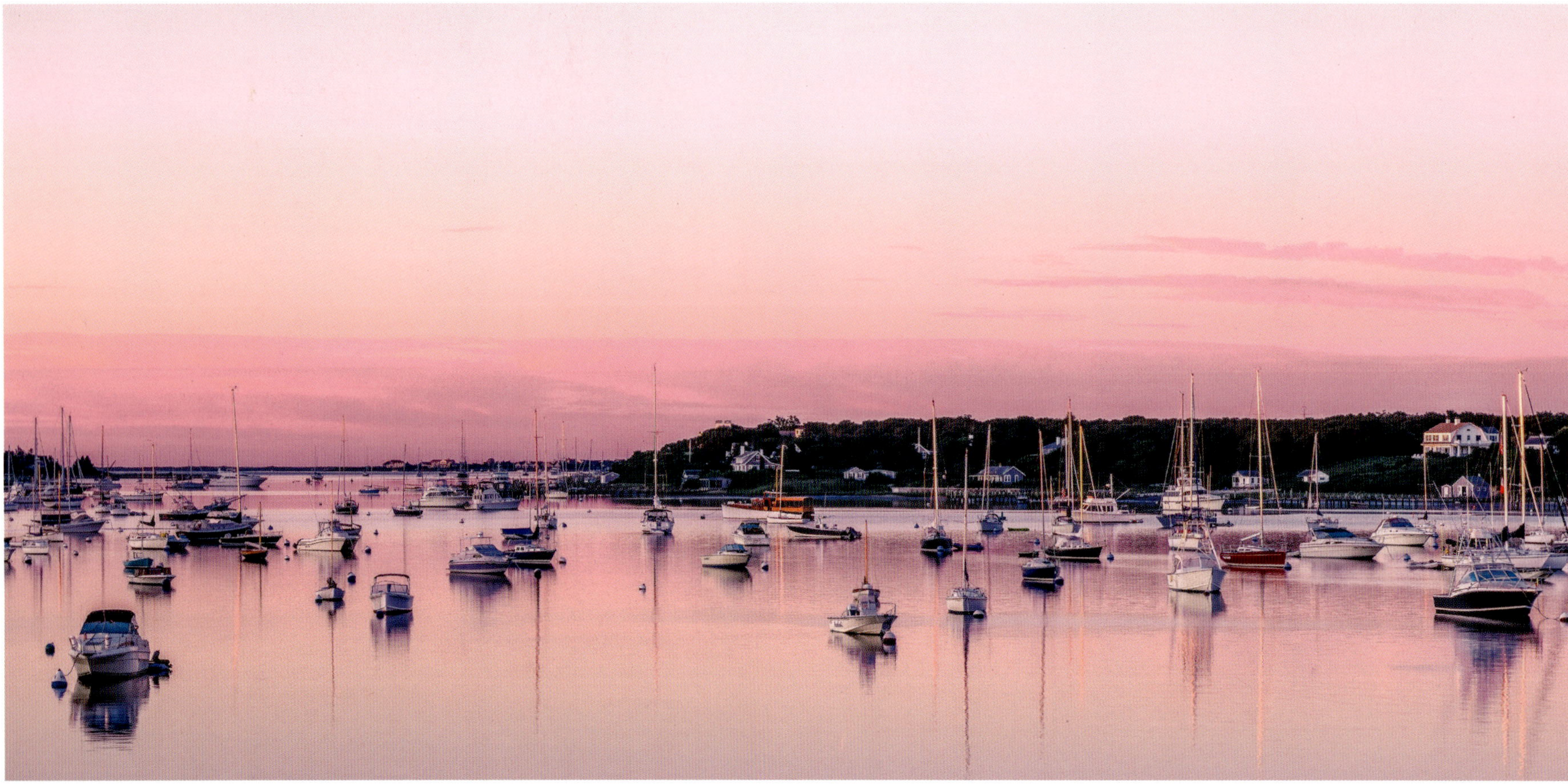

Inner Harbor

Edgartown

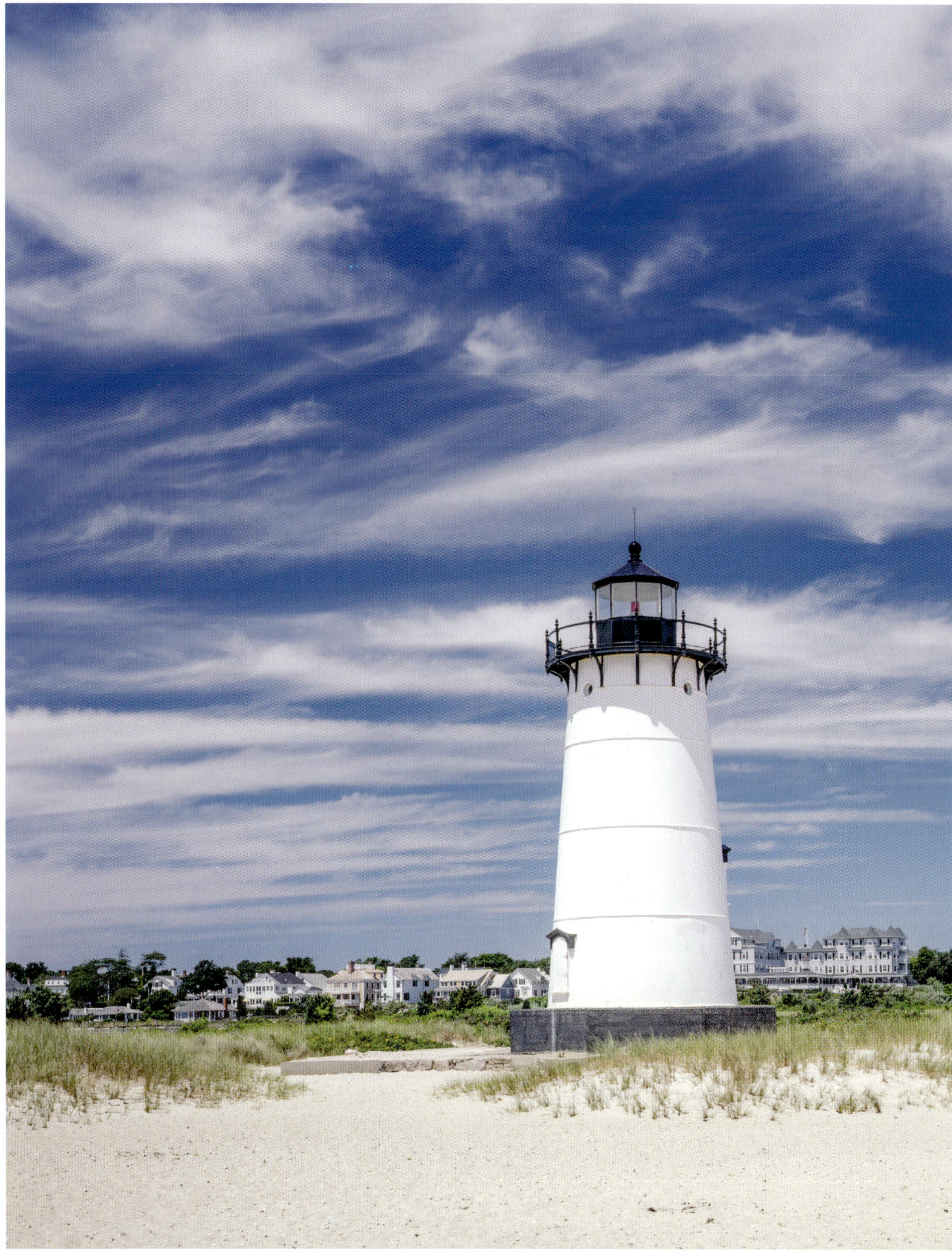

Cloud Swept Sands

Edgartown Lighthouse

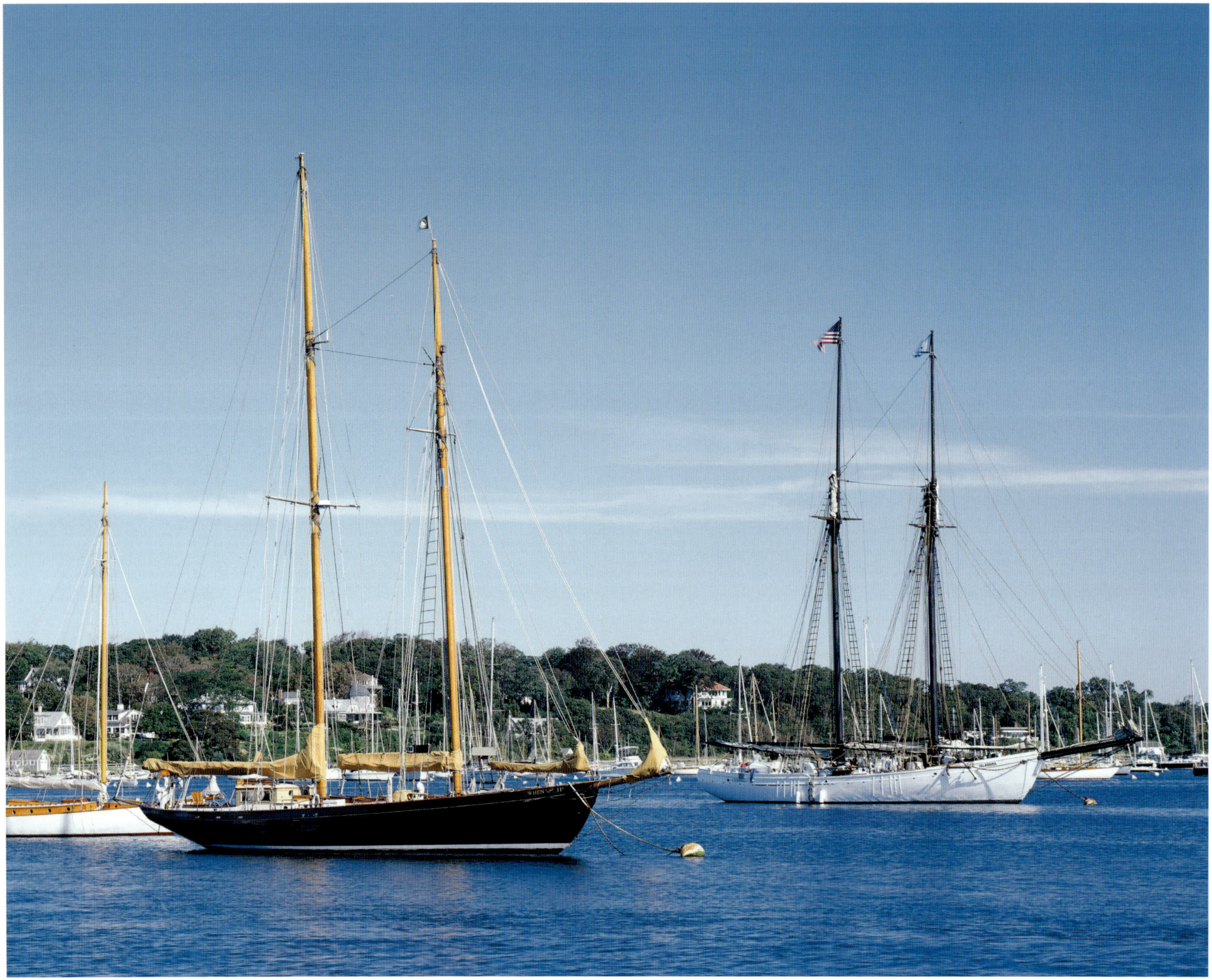

When and If, Alabama

Vineyard Haven Harbor

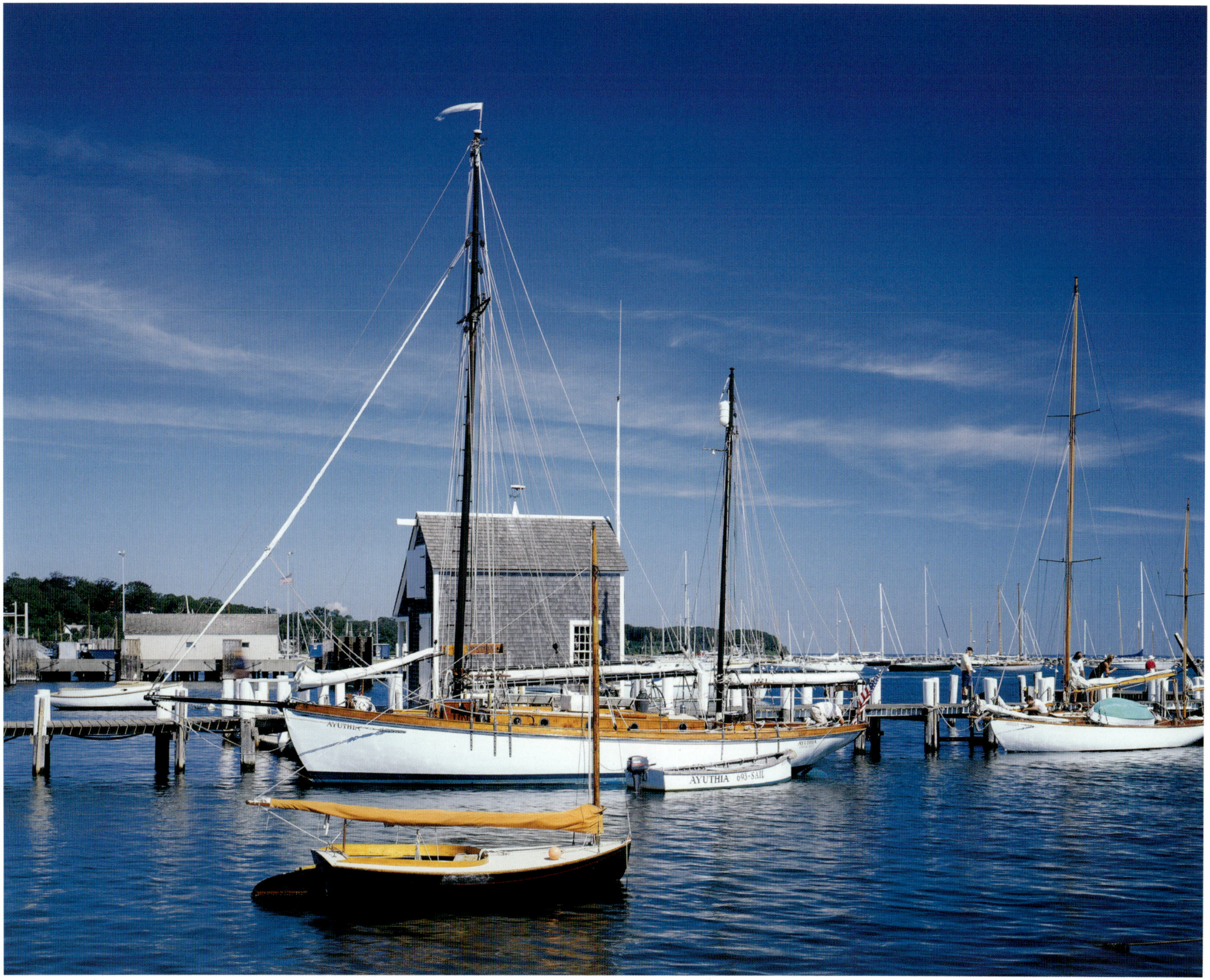

Ayuthia and Arabella

Vineyard Haven Harbor

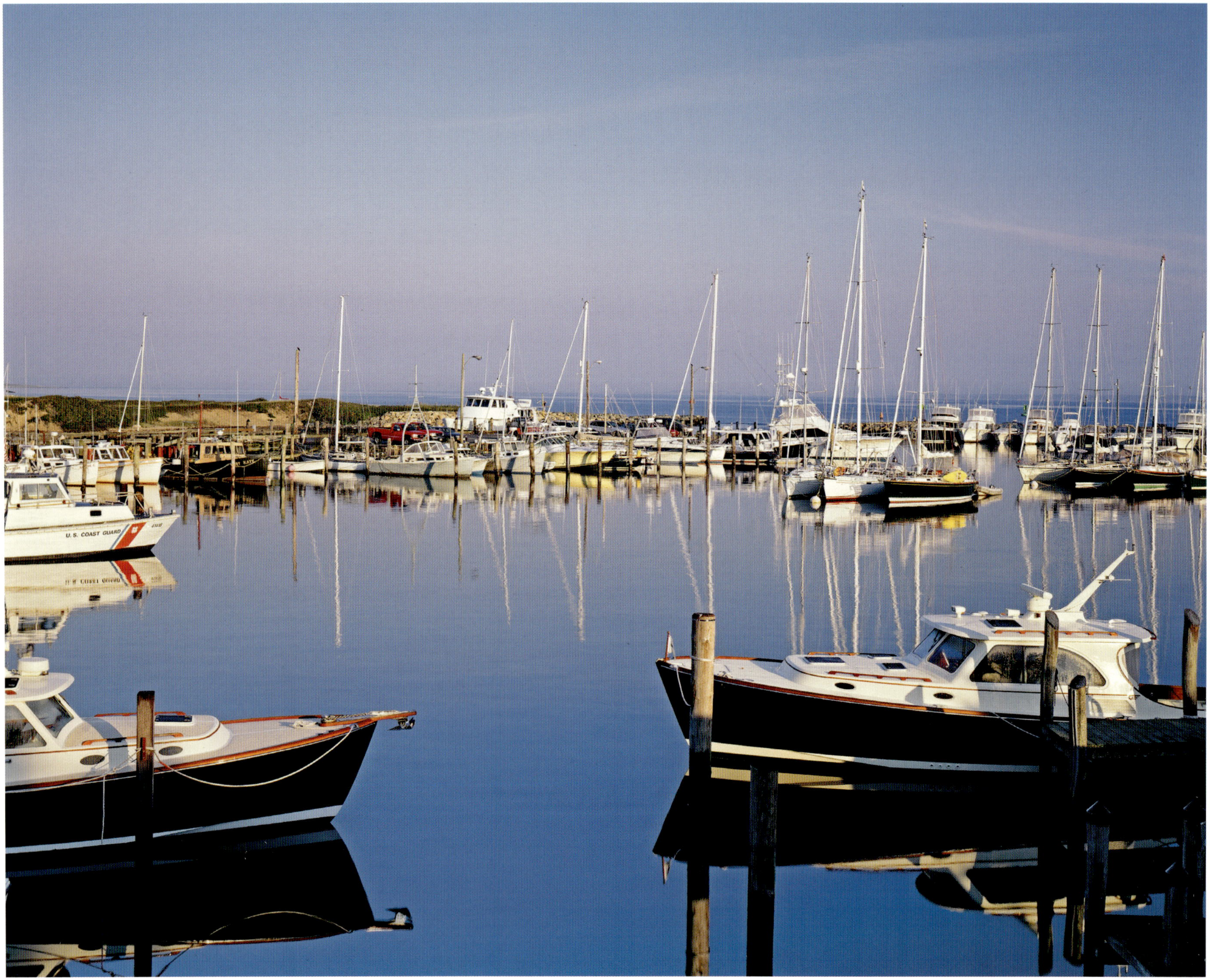

Hinckley Twins

Menemsha Harbor

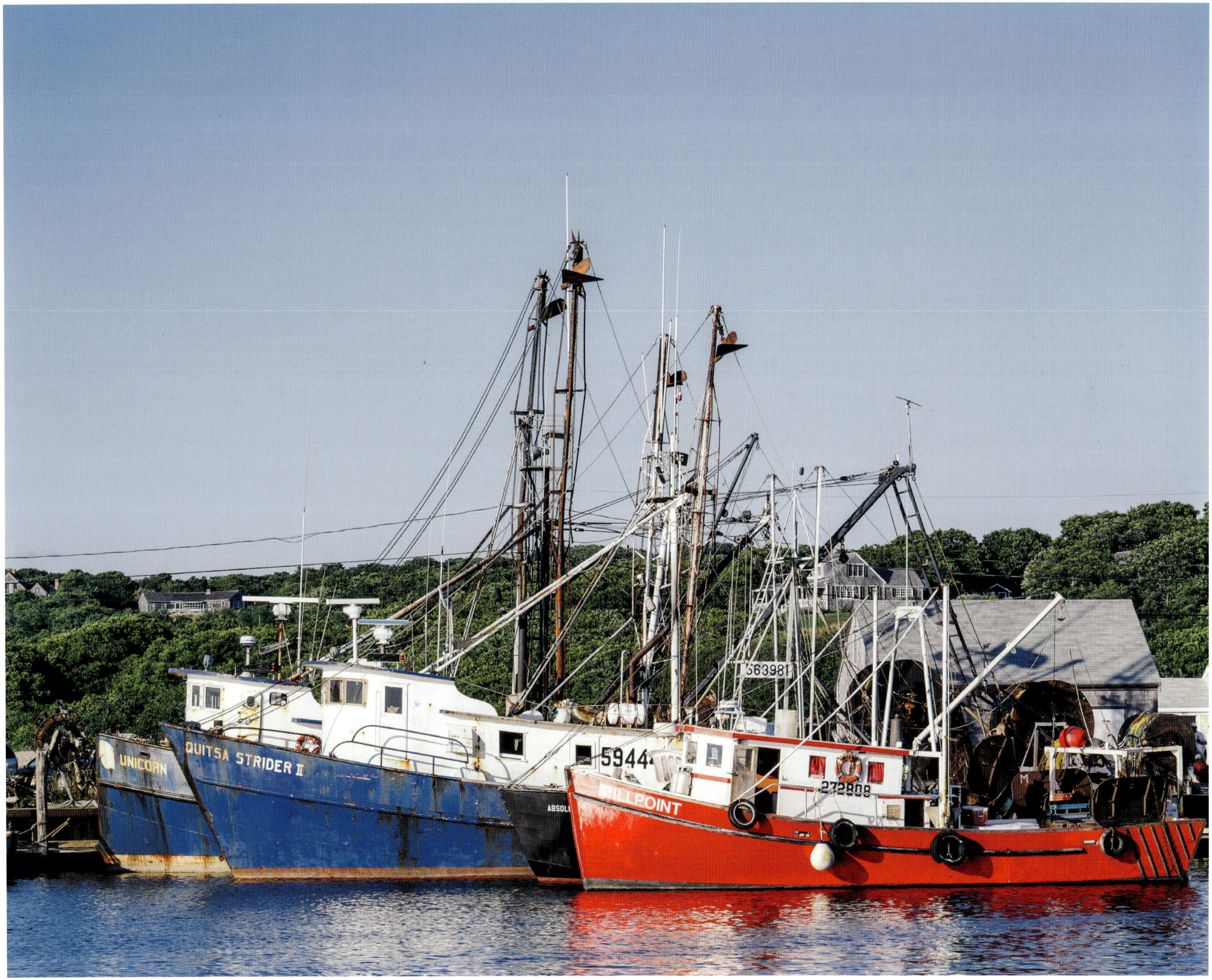

Fishing Fleet

Menemsha Harbor

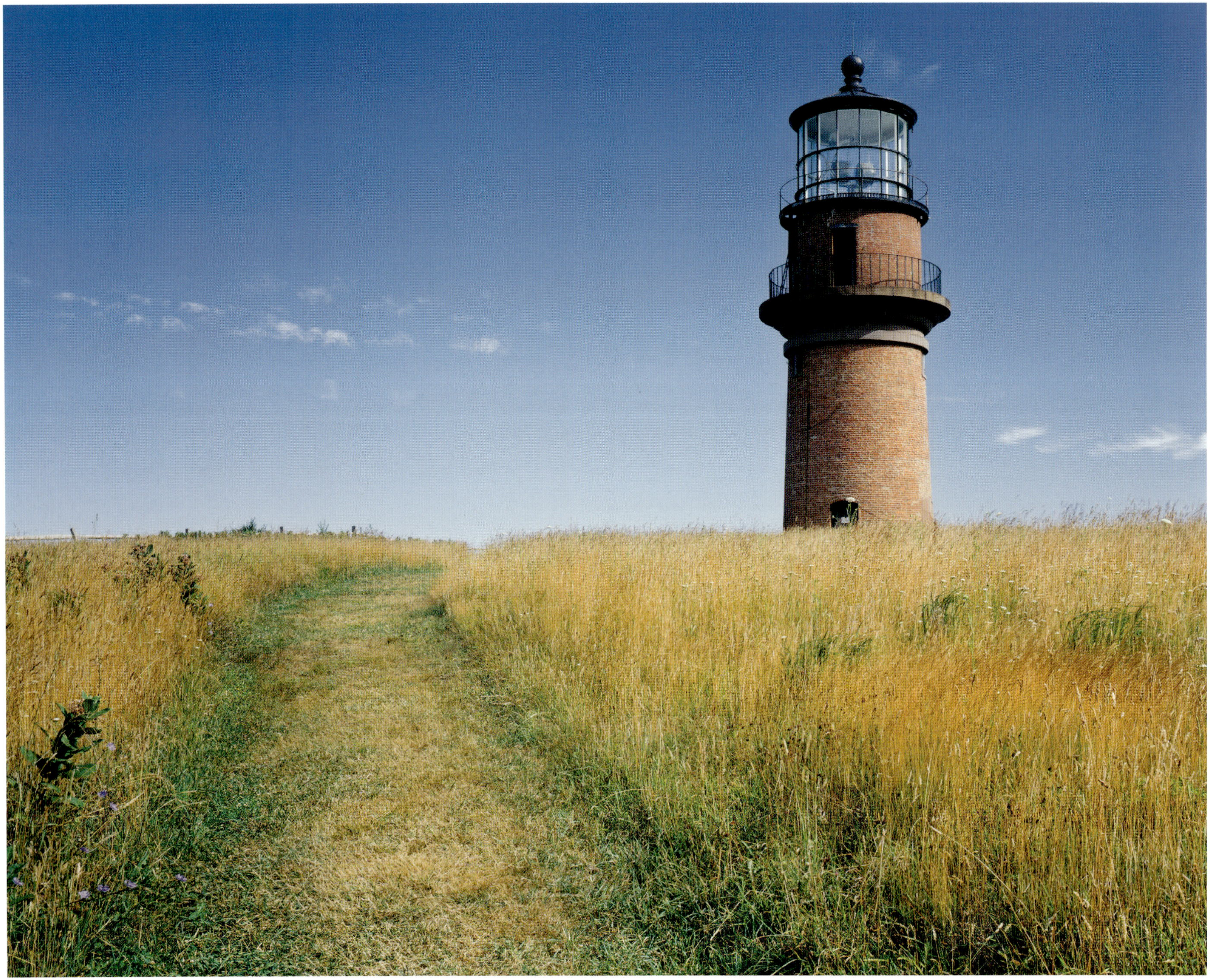

Summer Grass

Gay Head Lighthouse, Aquinnah

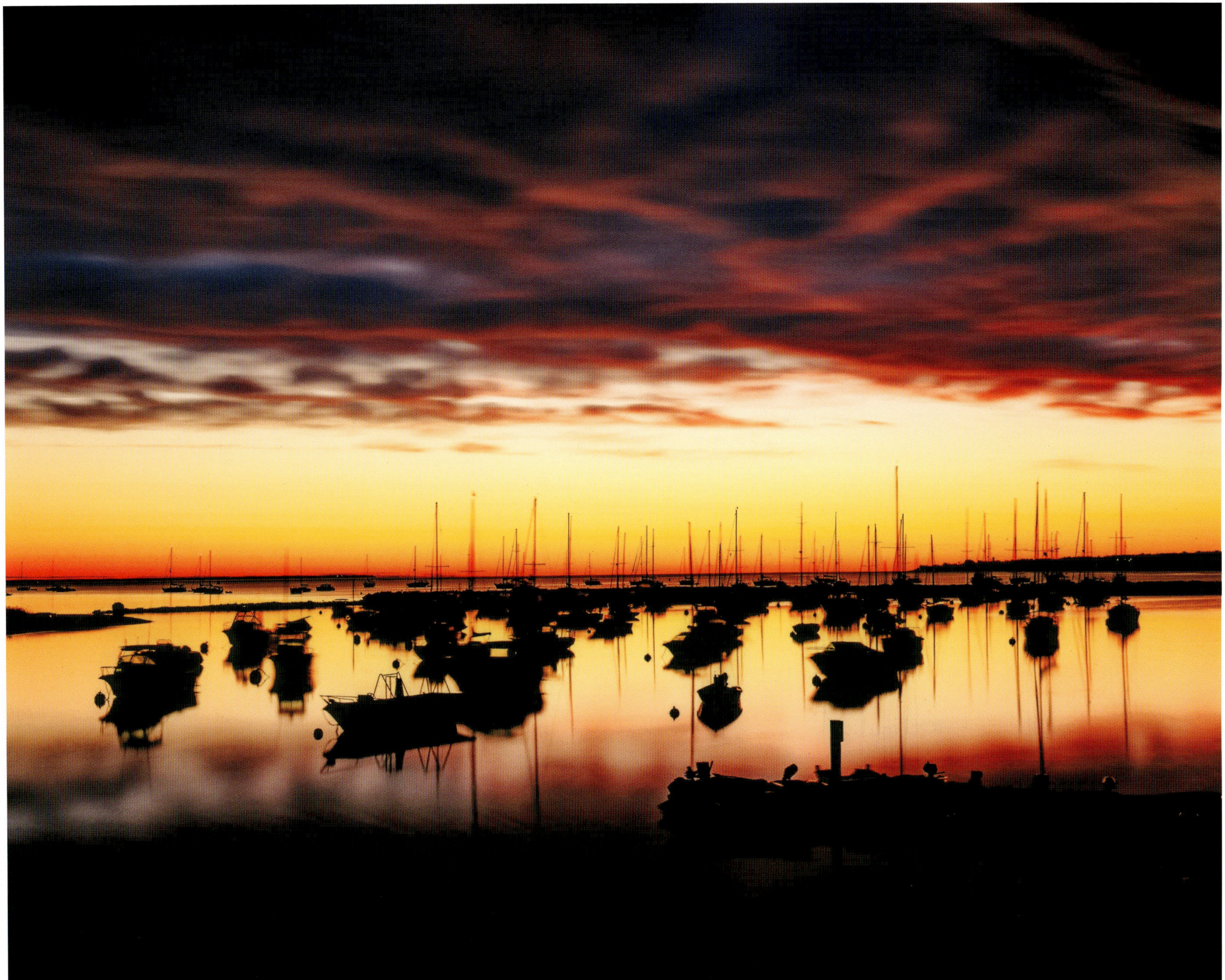

Sunrise Series I

Vineyard Haven Harbor

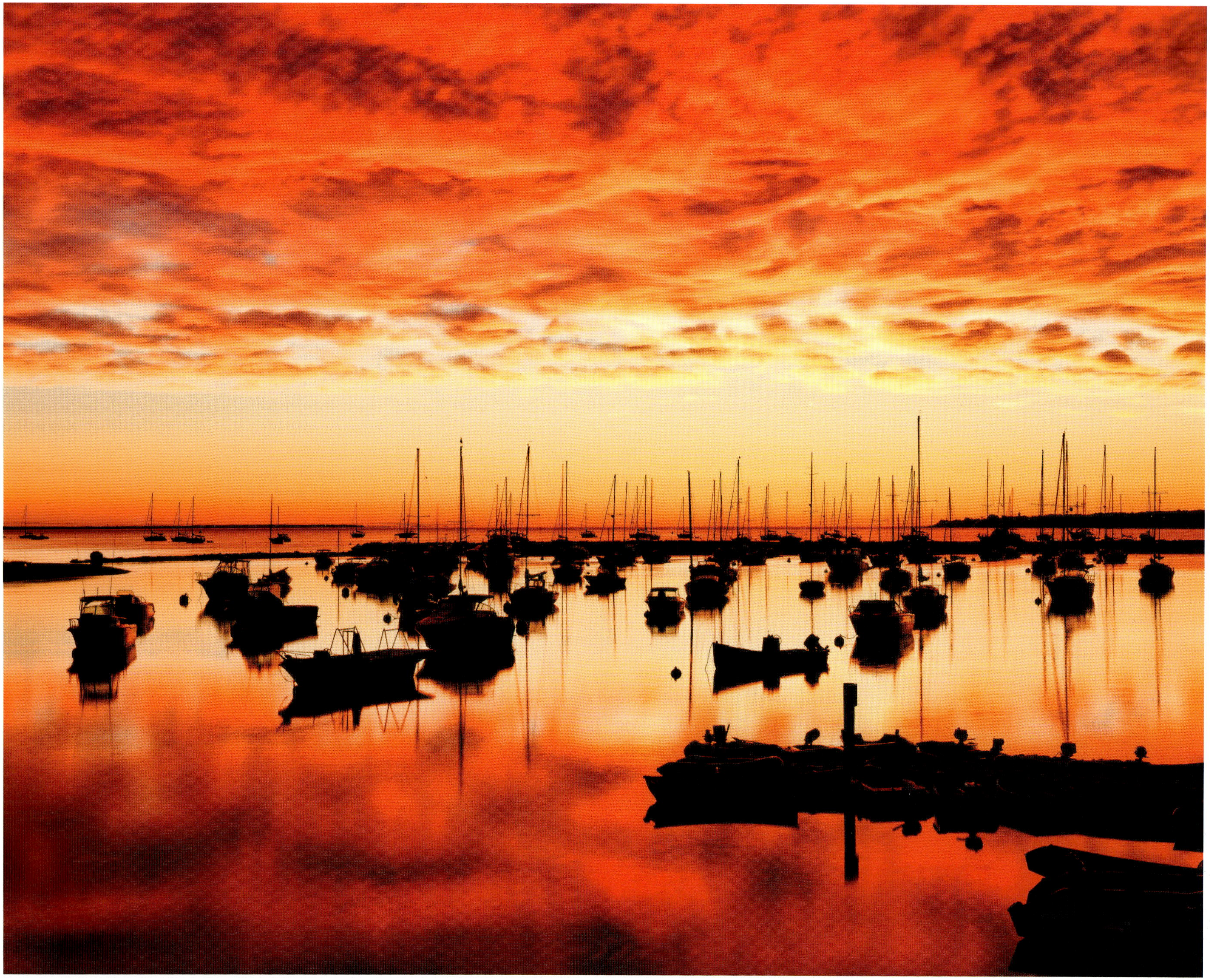

Sunrise Series 2

Vineyard Haven Harbor

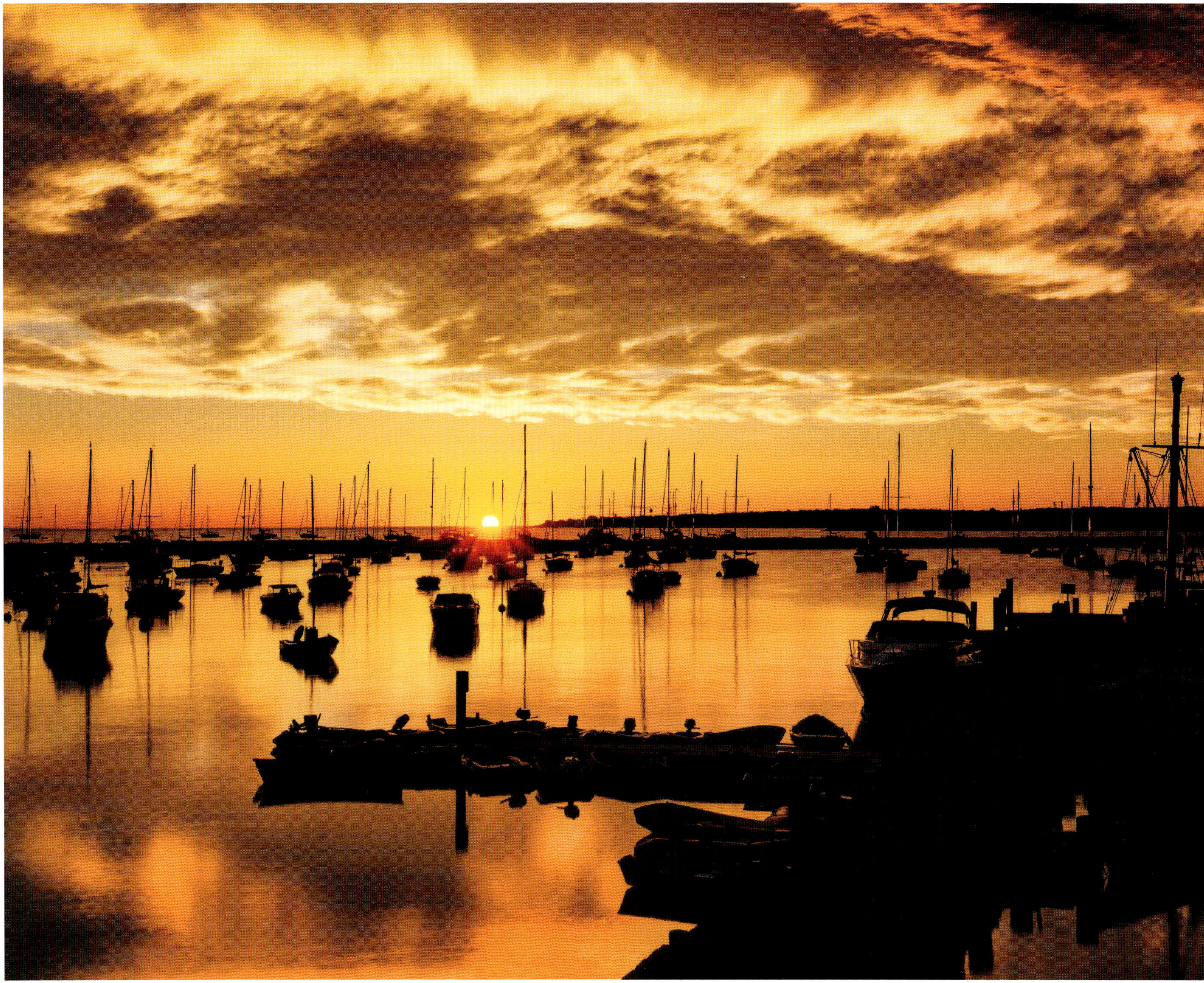

Sunrise Series 3 Vineyard Haven Harbor

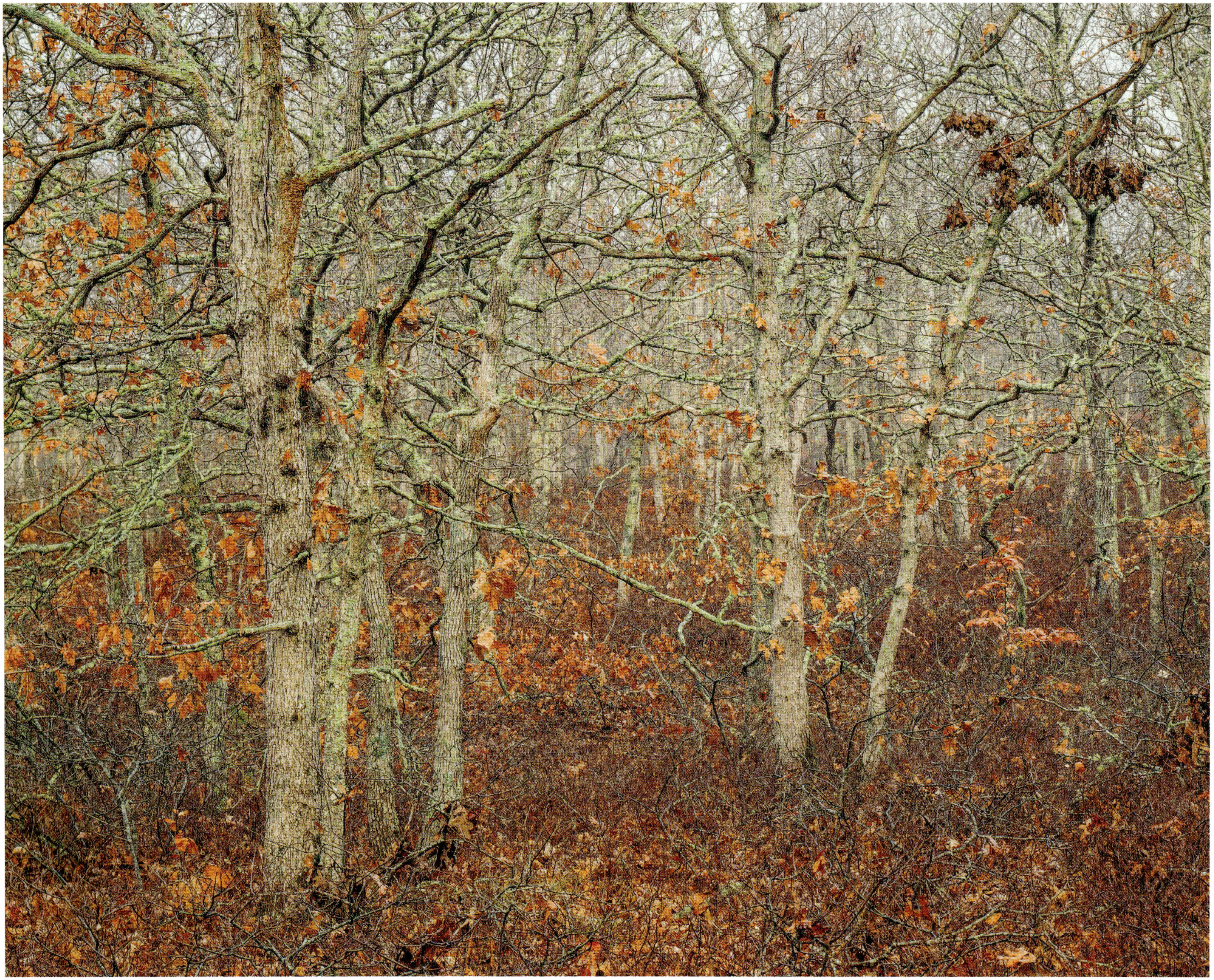

Oak Forest — West Tisbury

· FALL ·

WHERE HAVE ALL THE PEOPLE GONE? FALL IS THE favorite time of the year for many people who love the Vineyard. Summer is too short, but Vineyarders do their best to stretch it into fall. The color changes of autumn are subtle, but no less beautiful. By the time the leaves drop, you've forgotten that they were once green. Houses that have been obscured by summer growth are visible again, and vistas of the sound and the ocean open and expand. Outdoor activities continue long into the fall, even after most of the summer people have returned to their off-season homes. Some year-rounders, stressed-out and overworked by summer, enjoy their first chance to visit the beach. It is much quieter there now, and dogs are welcome. It's time for the fishing derby, then it's hunting season! Schools open and summer businesses begin to close. Foghorns are heard more frequently as clouds seem to get fuller and drop lower in the sky. Sunset comes earlier, but its palette of colors expands dramatically. The boat schedules change. There are fewer trips, and the Steamship Authority ferries to Oak Bluffs stop entirely. Fishermen ready foul weather gear as they head to richer fishing grounds farther offshore, and carpenters begin wearing layers of clothes. Lawn mowers are stored away, garden hoses coiled, and farmers change course as their fields and gardens are put to bed. There's time now to reflect on the summer just past.

— *T.O.*

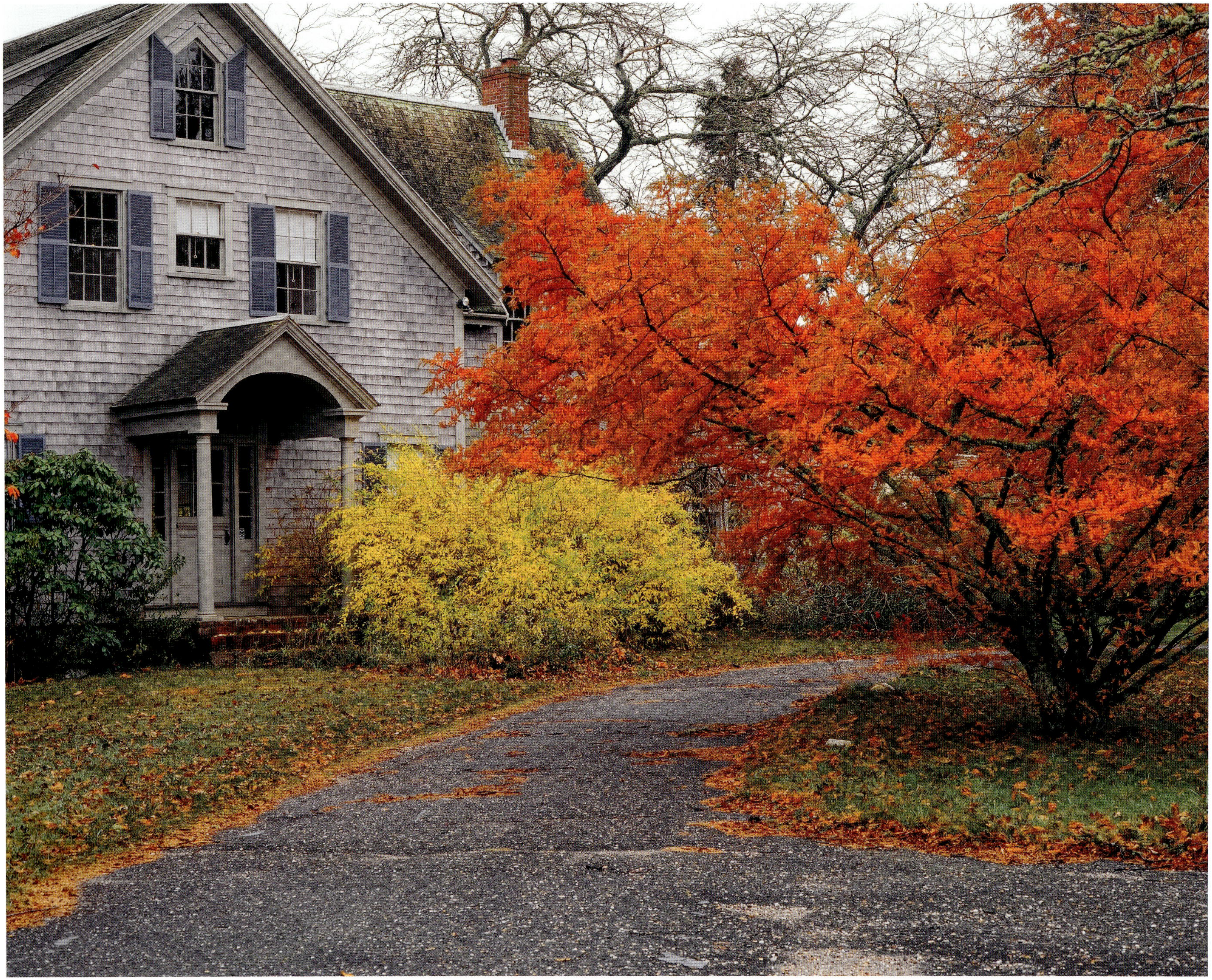

New Color Chilmark

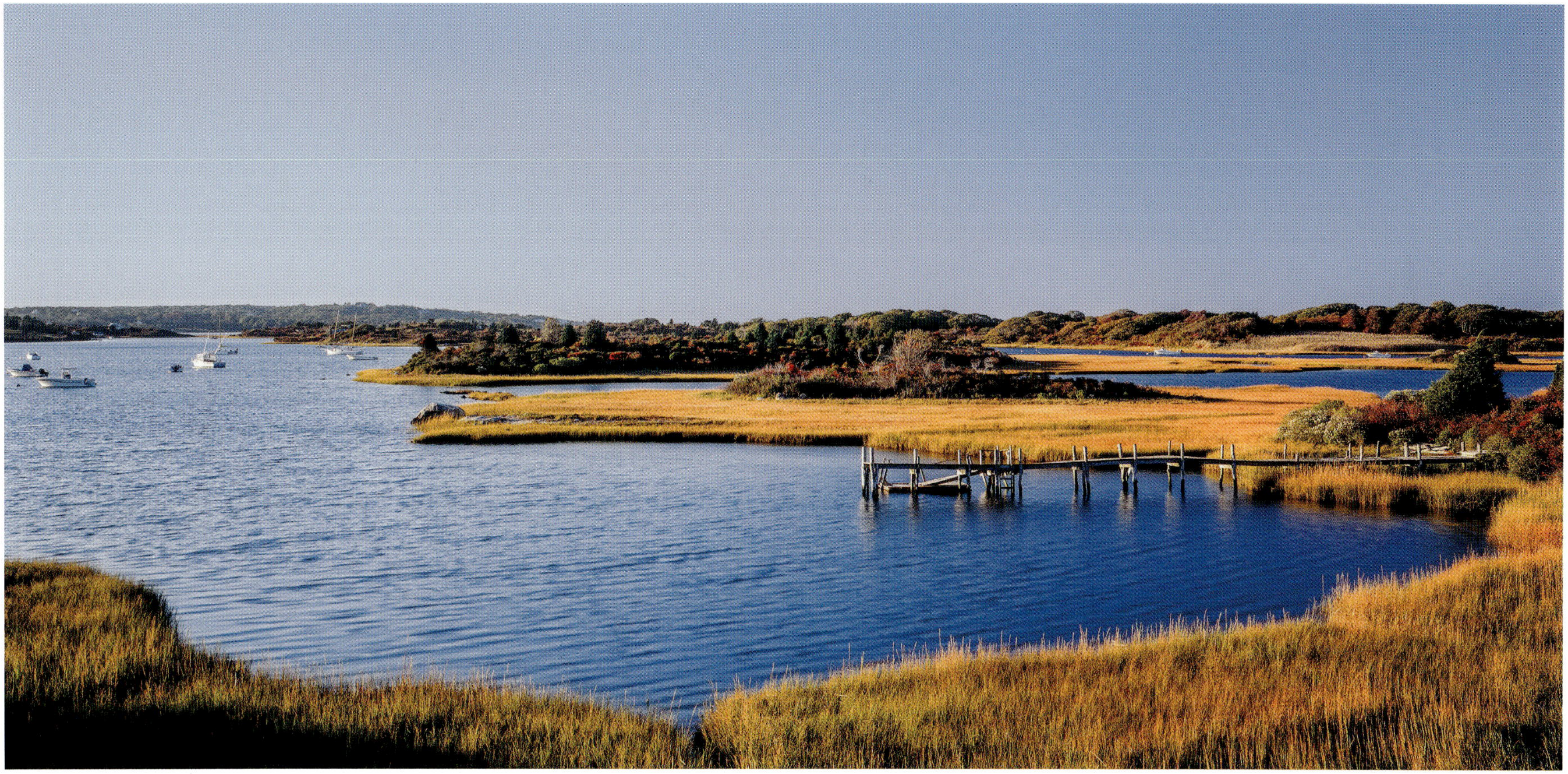

Empty Dock Chilmark

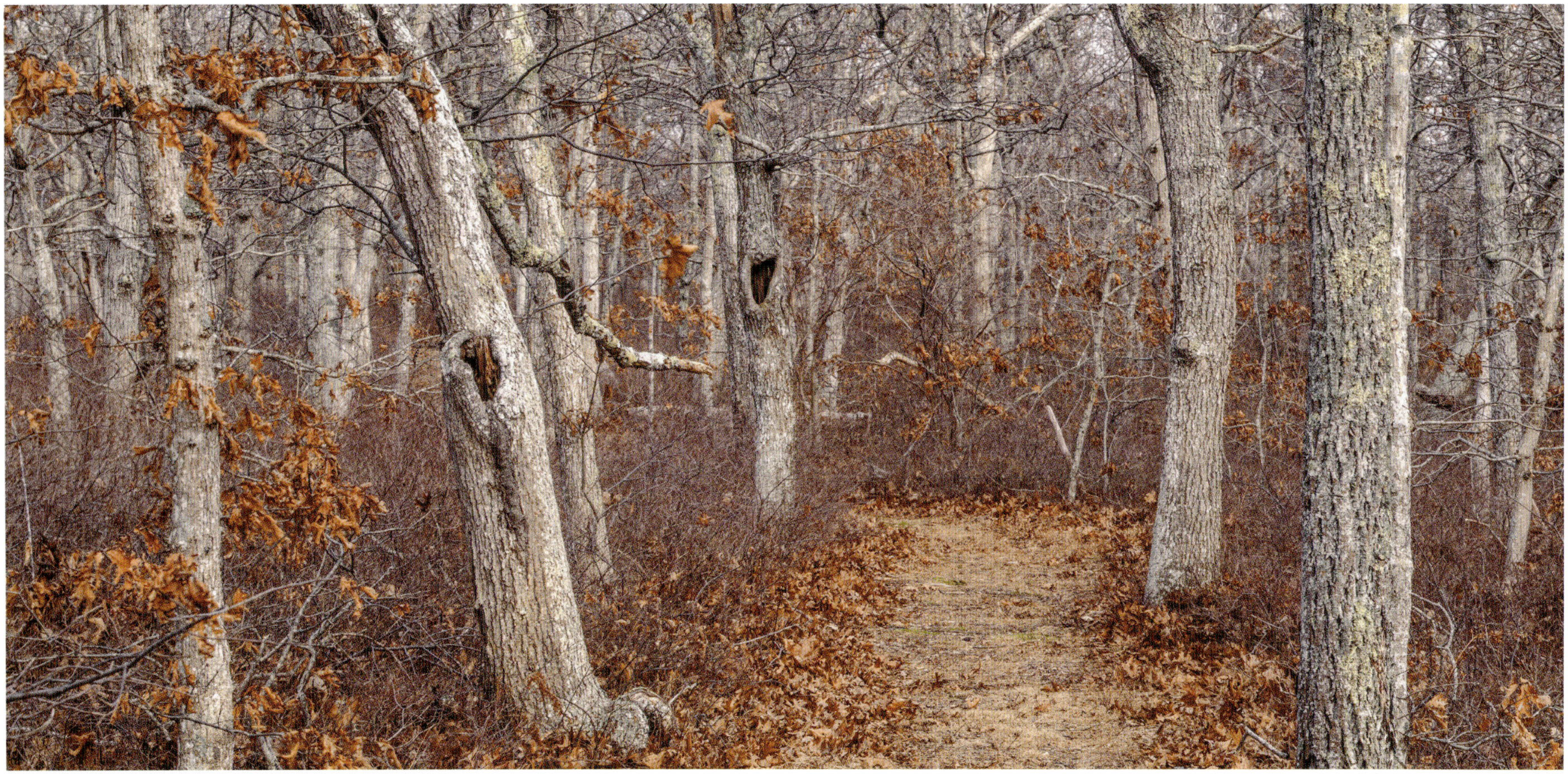

Leaves on the Trail — Long Point Refuge

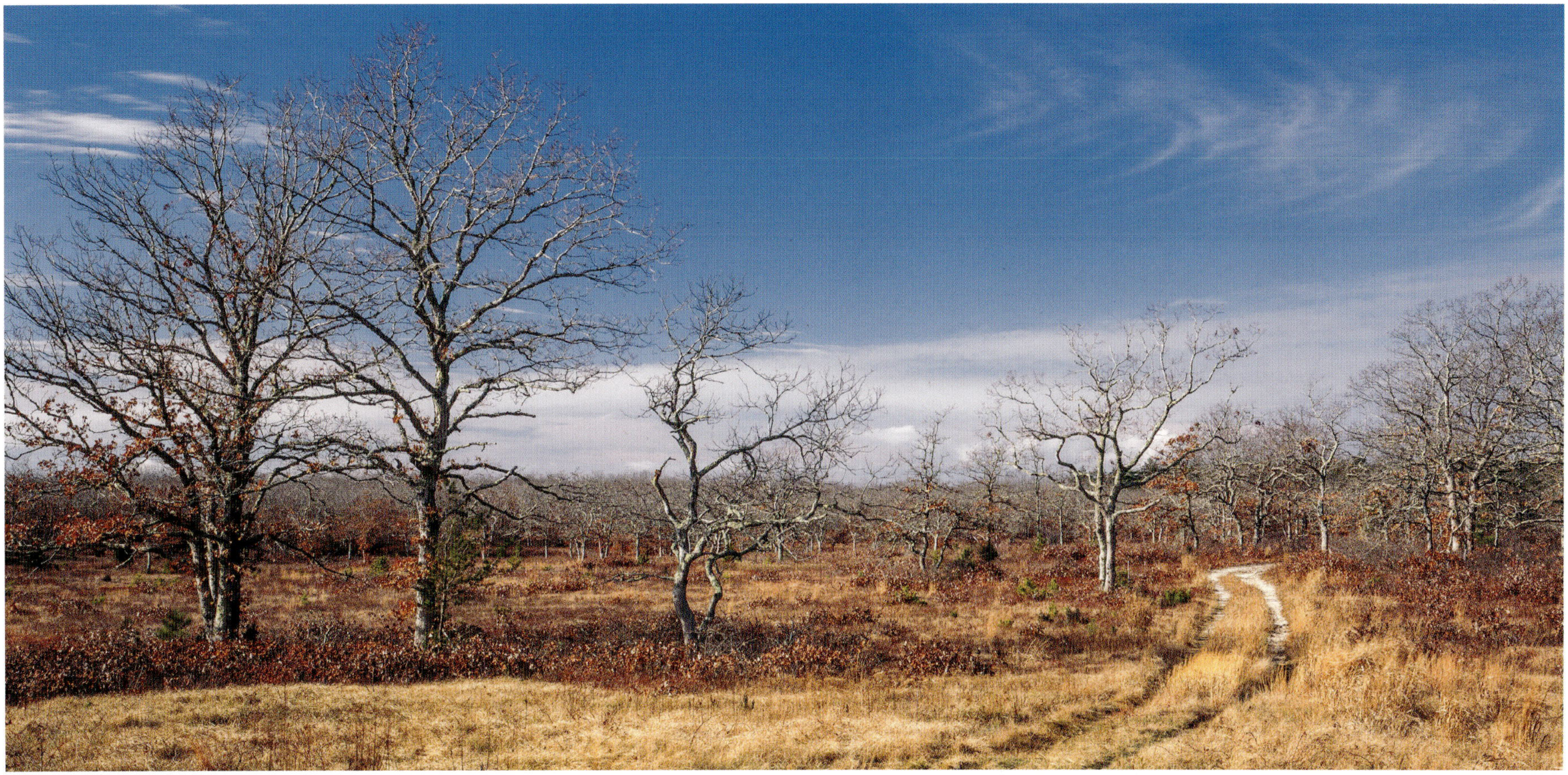

Sandy Track

Manuel F. Correllus State Forest

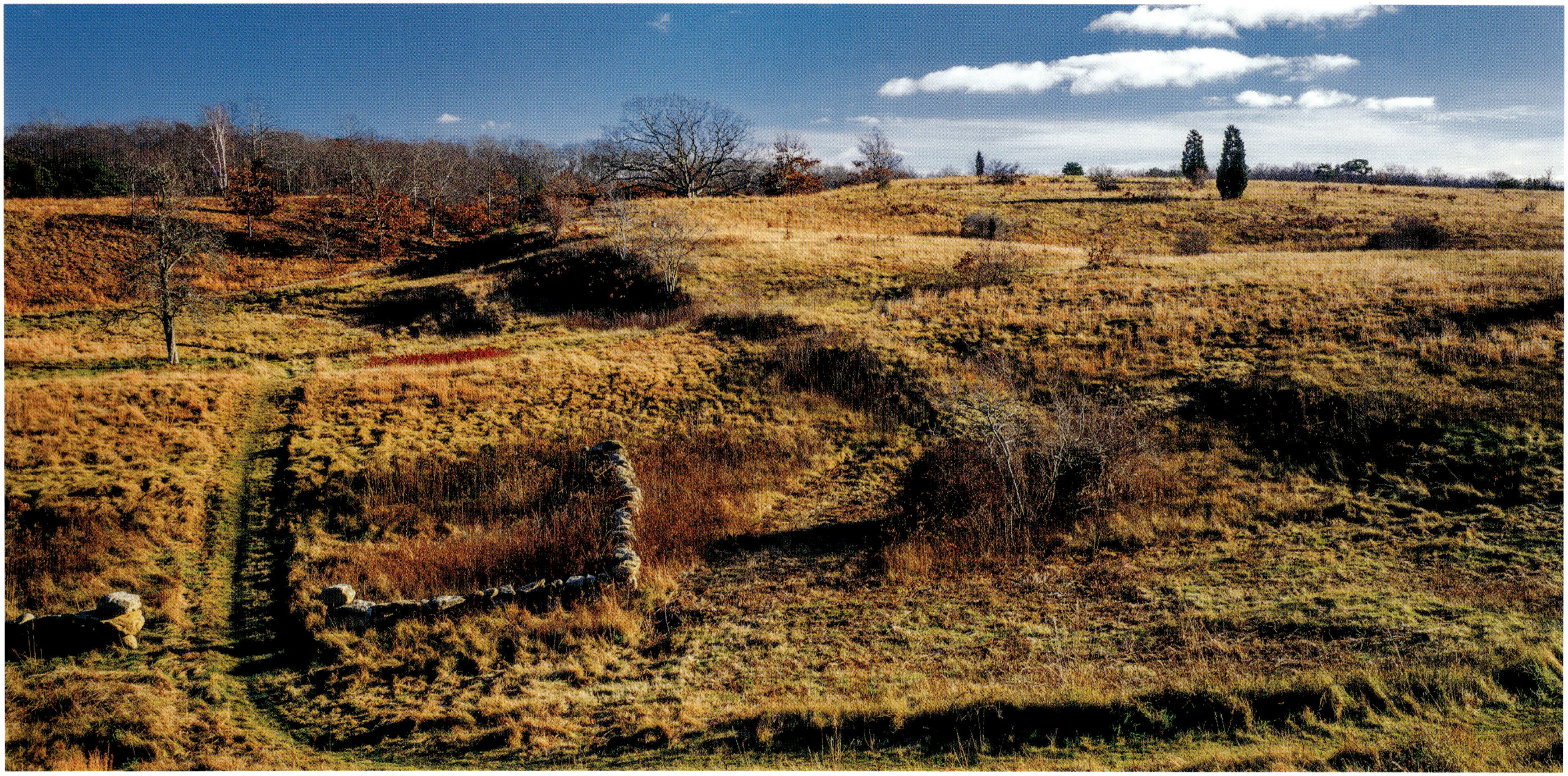

Stone Walls

Tisbury

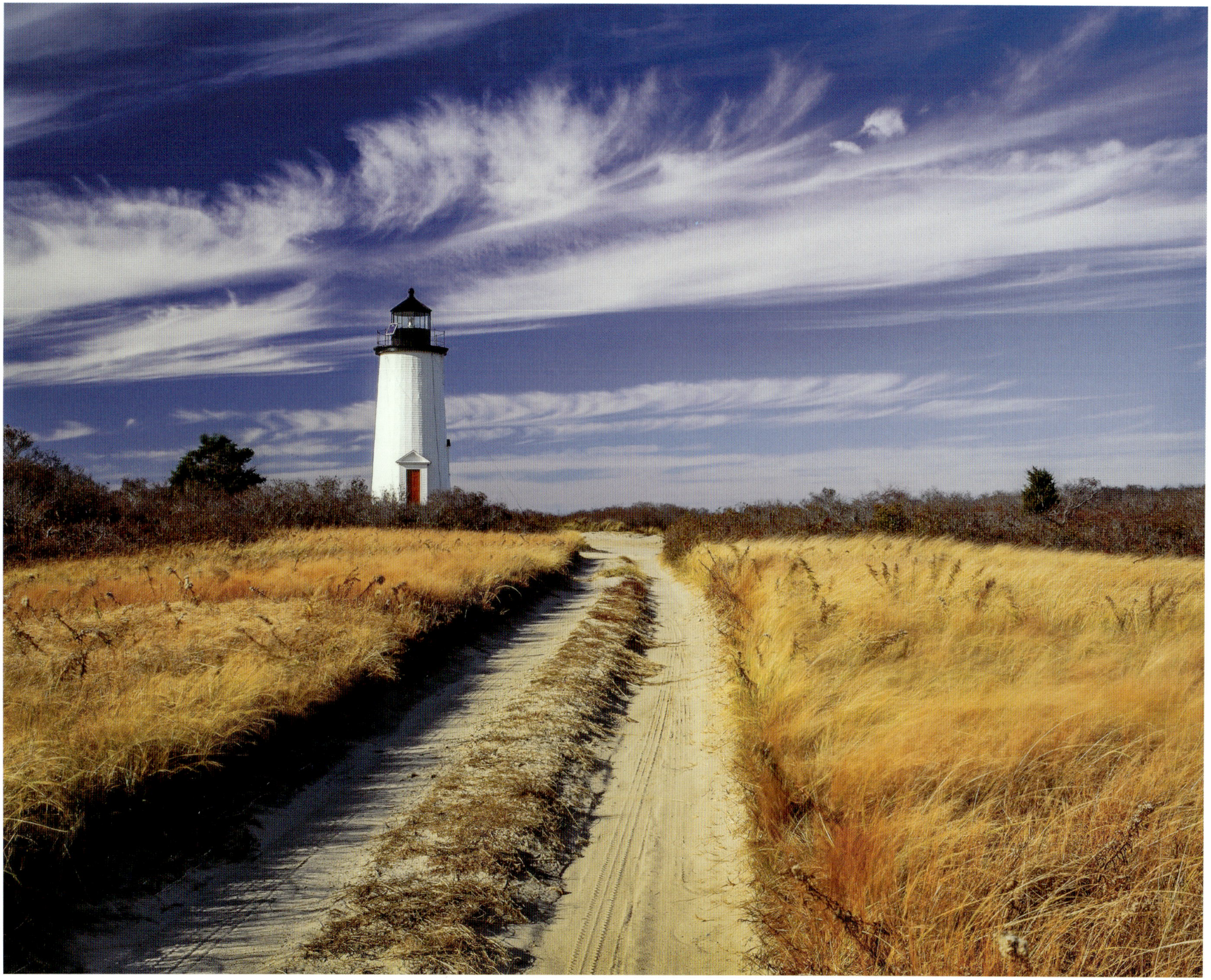

Windswept Grass

Cape Poge Lighthouse

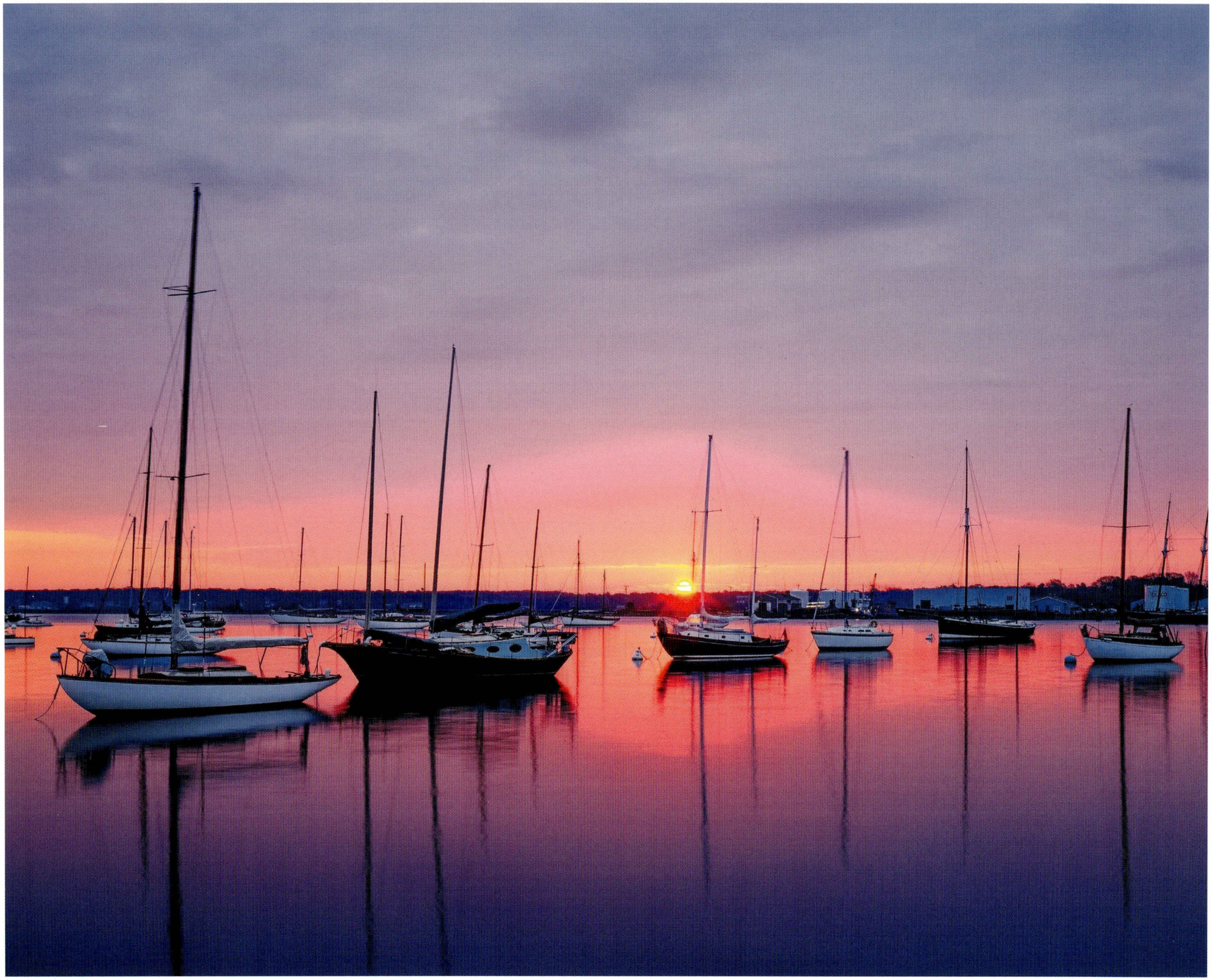

Ready to Haul

Vineyard Haven Harbor

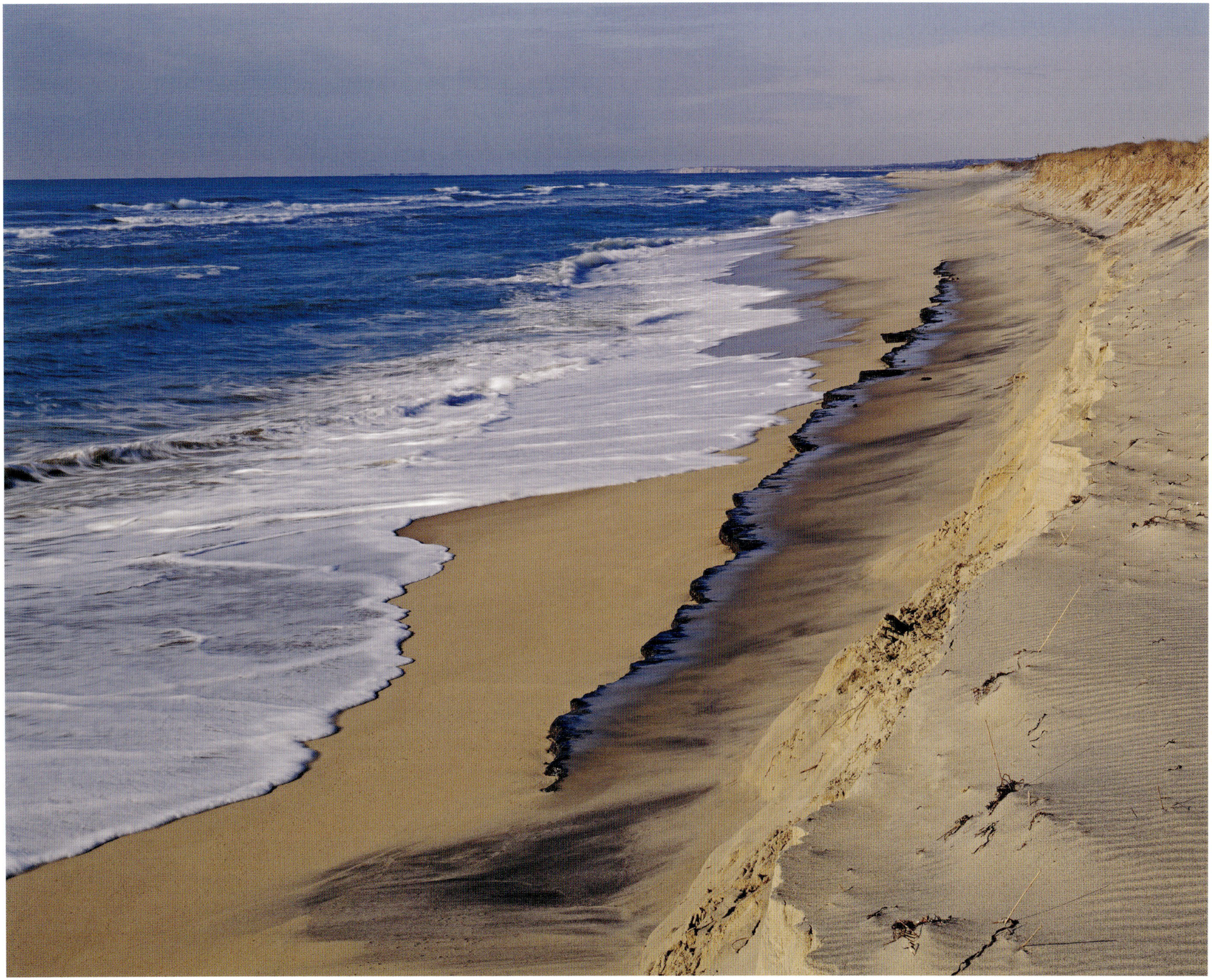

Cliff Walk

South Beach, Edgartown

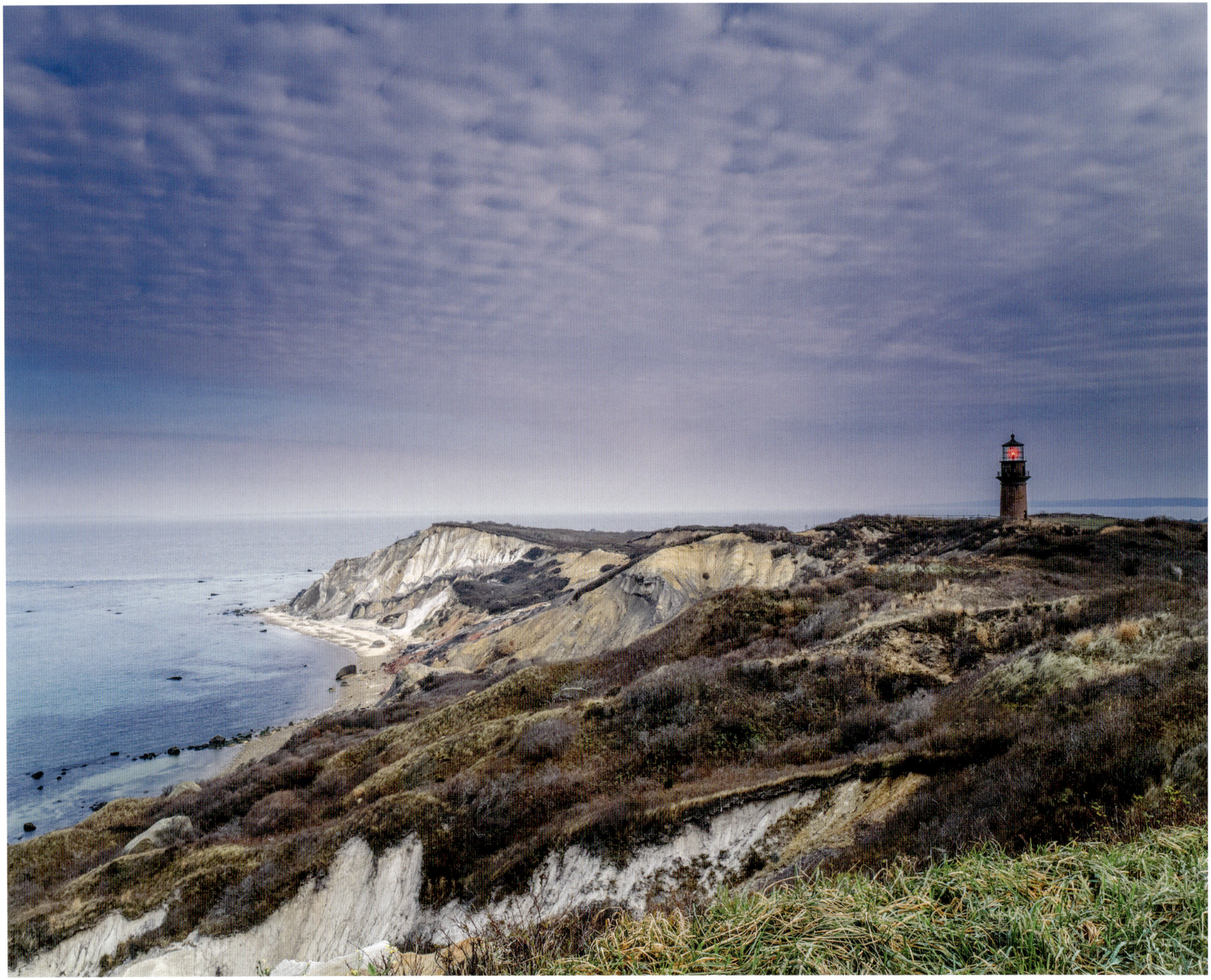

Northwest Horizon

Gay Head Lighthouse, Aquinnah

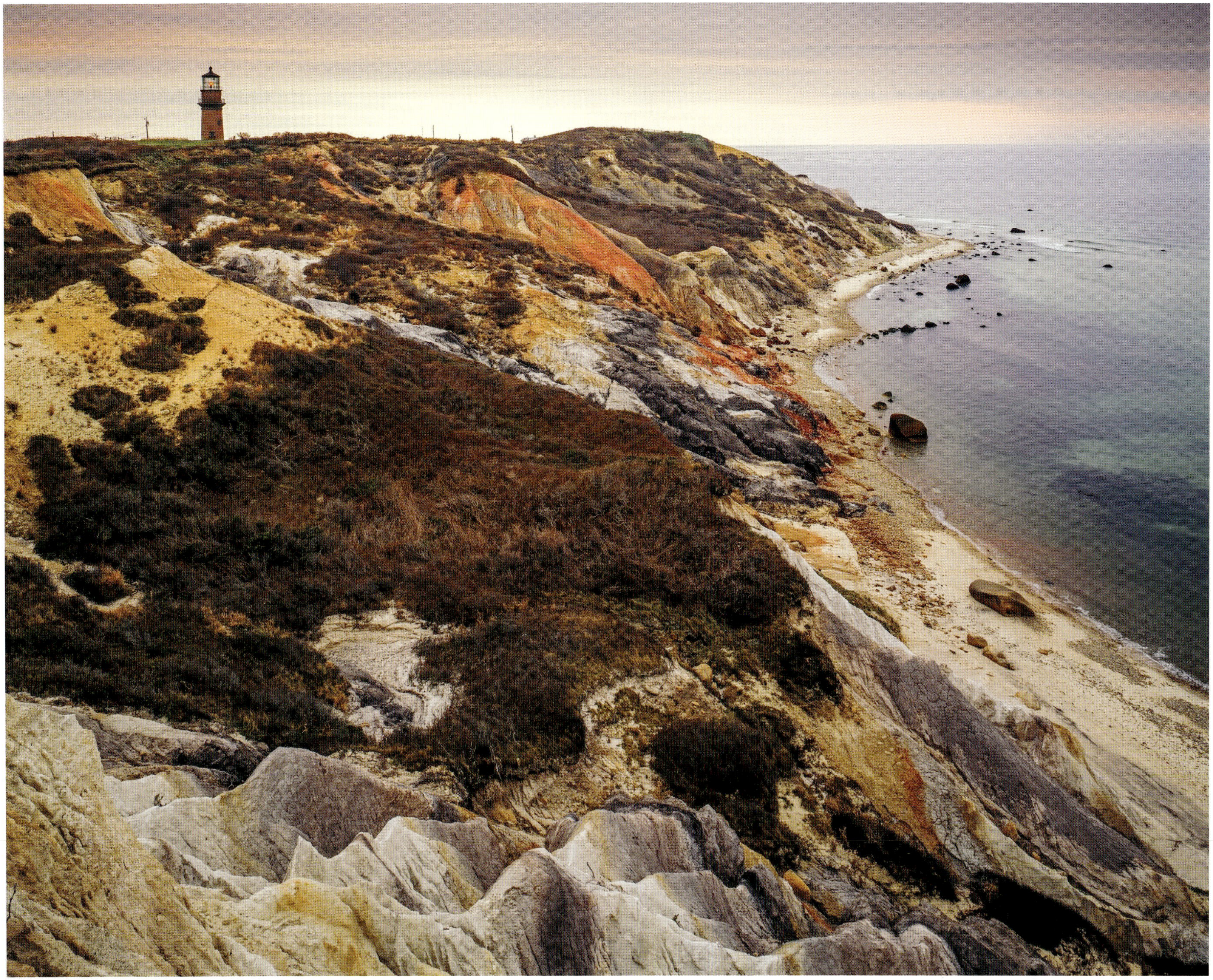

Southwest Horizon Gay Head Lighthouse, Aquinnah

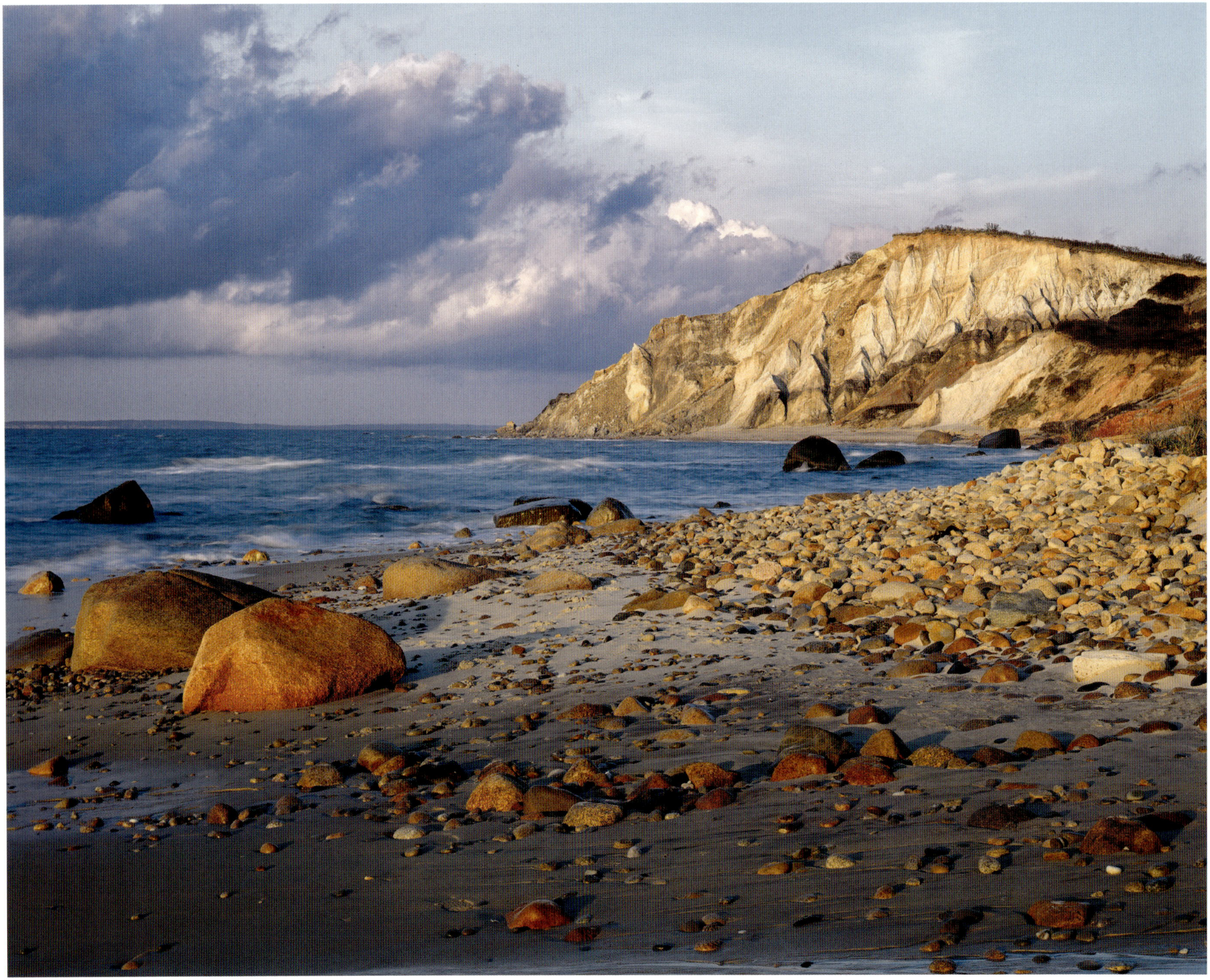

Rocky Beach

Gay Head Cliffs, Aquinnah

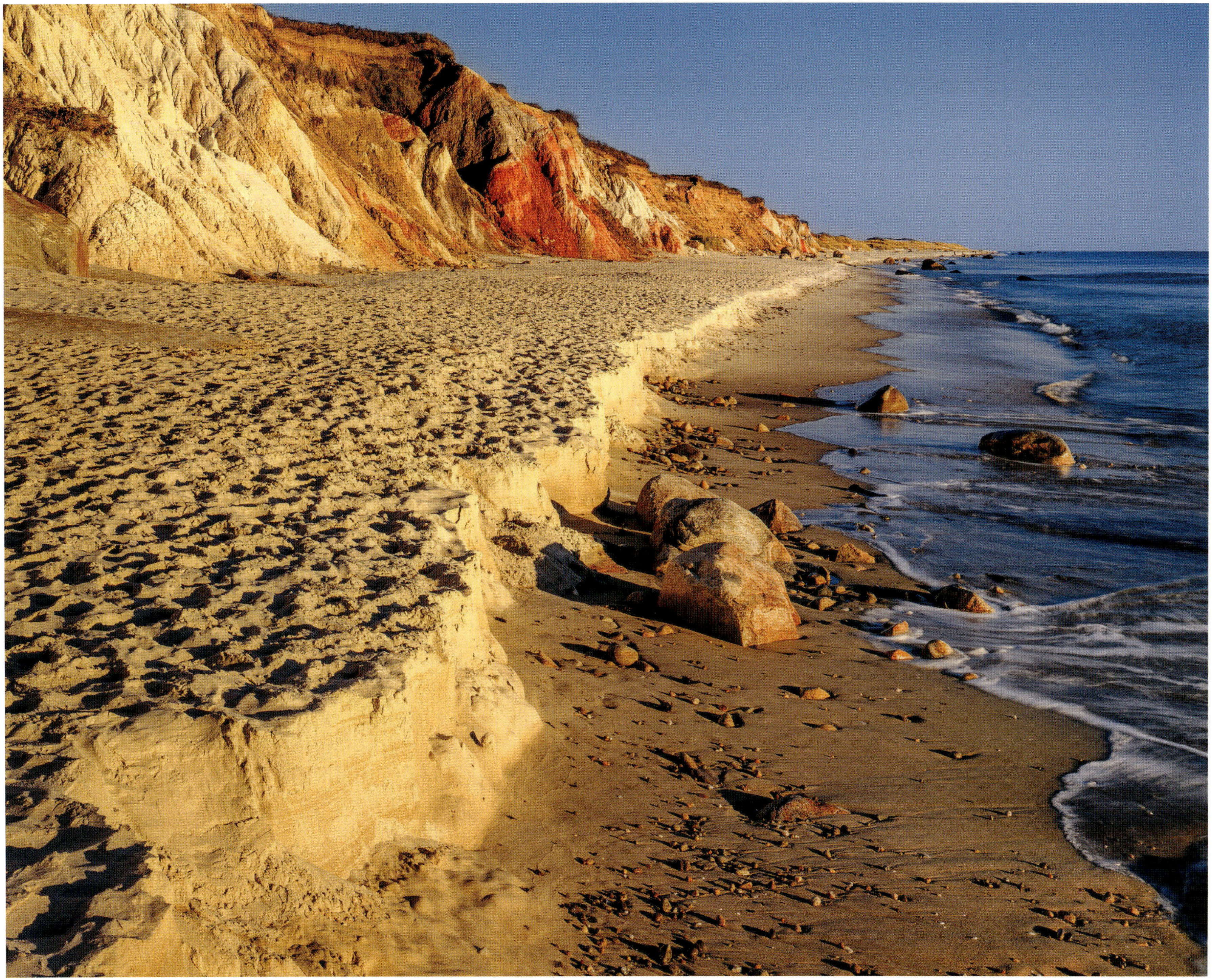

Swept to Sea

Moshup Beach, Aquinnah

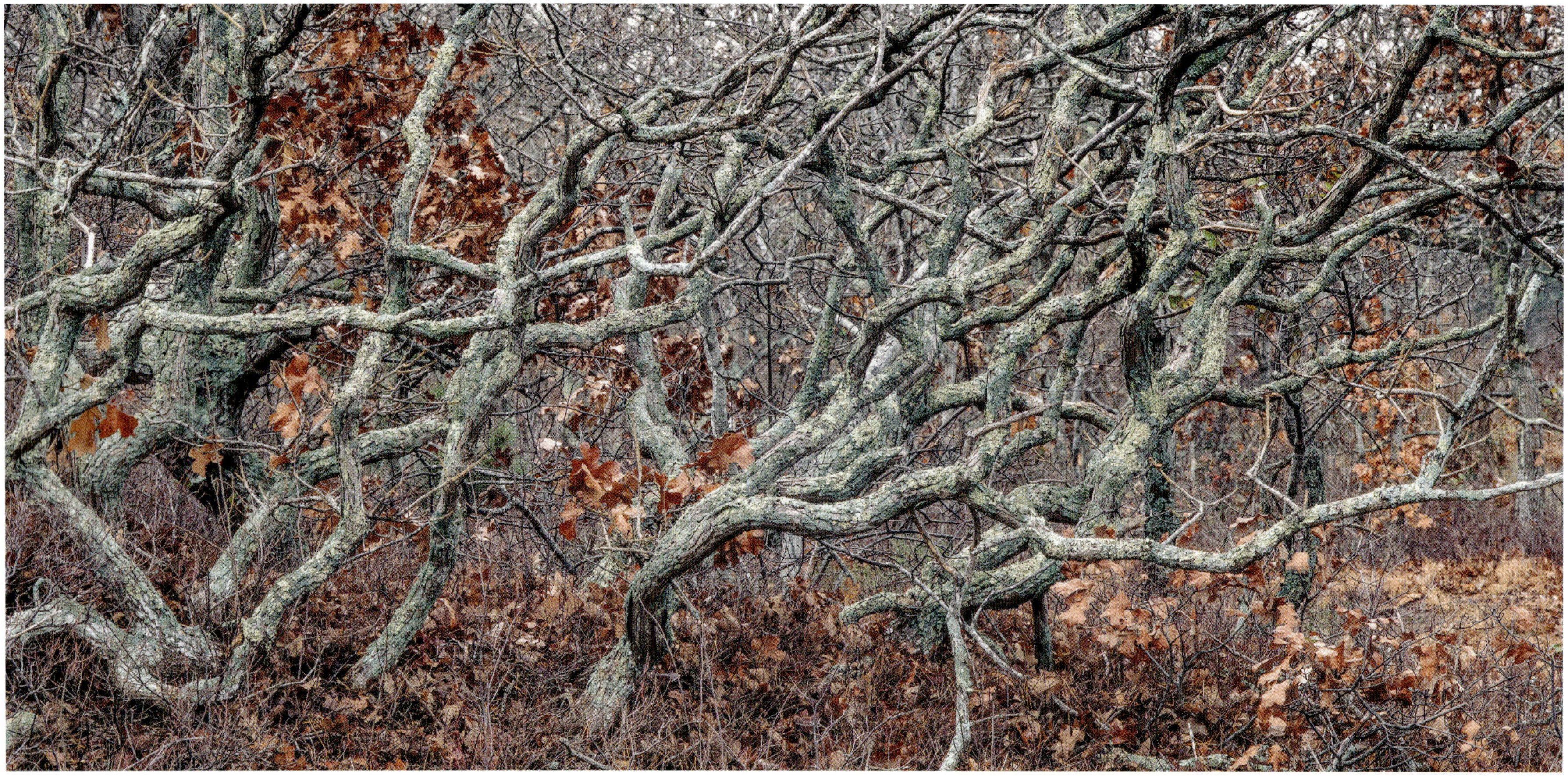

Oaks Intertwined | Chappaquiddick

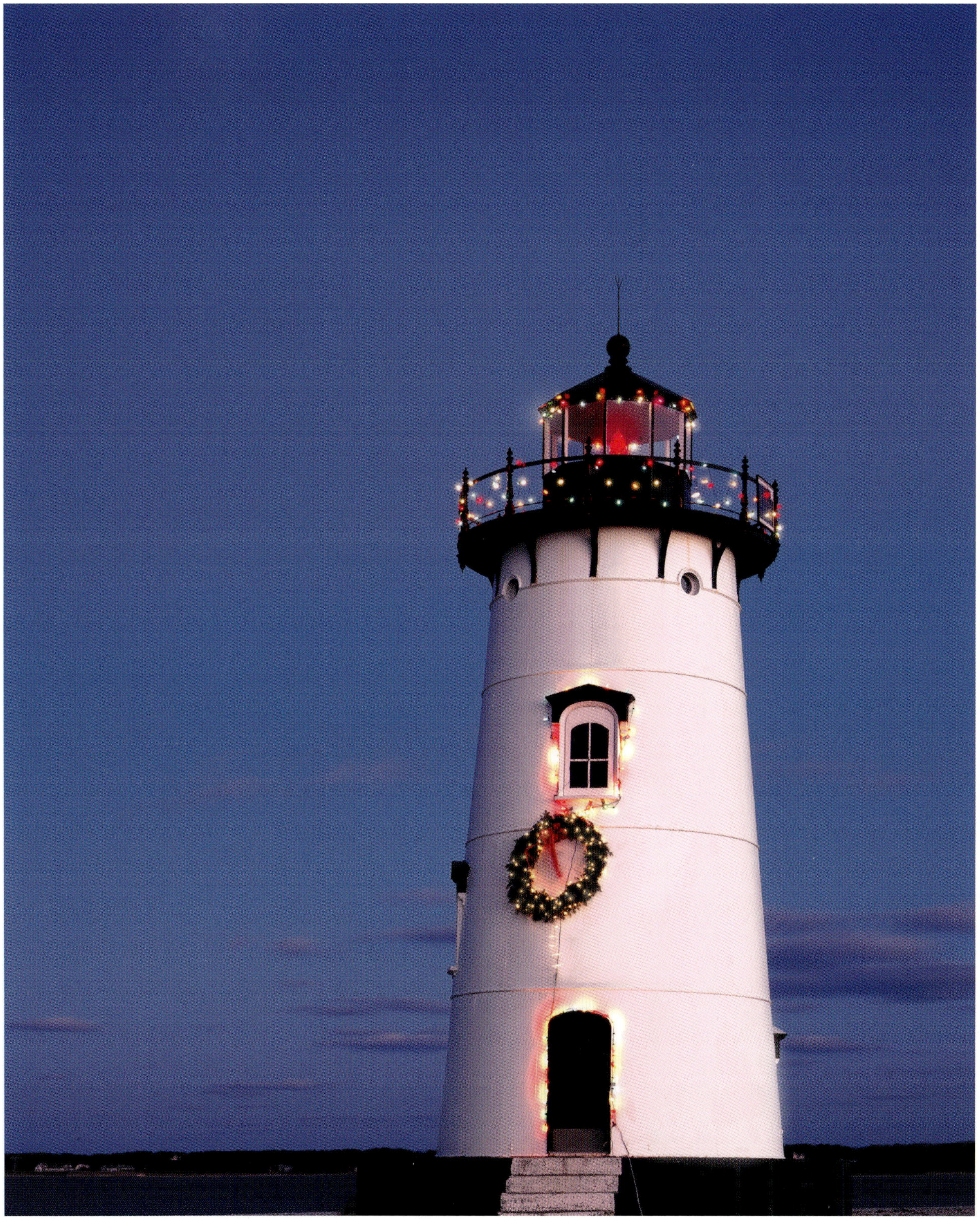

Season of Light

Edgartown Lighthouse

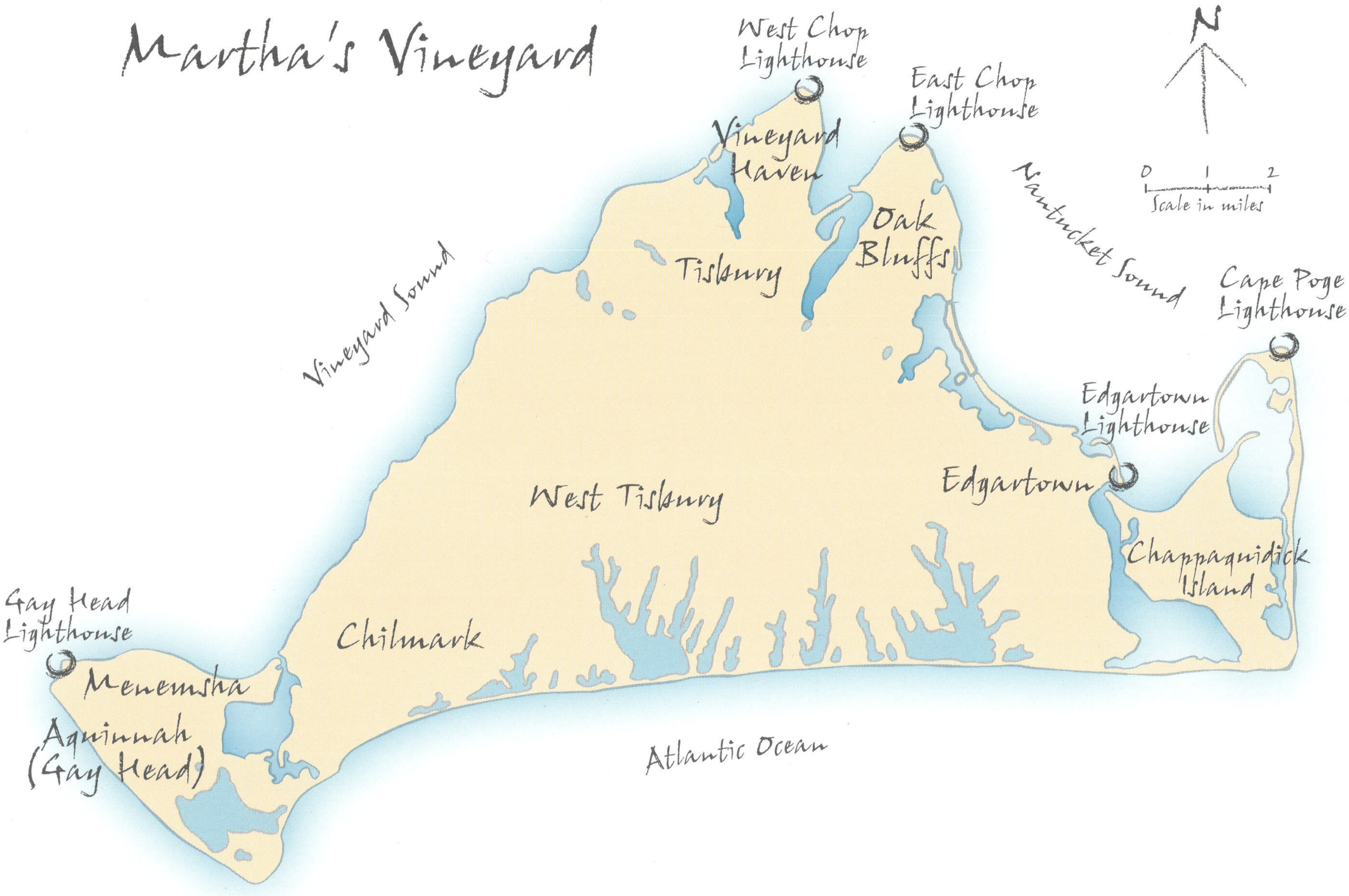
Martha's Vineyard
West Chop Lighthouse
East Chop Lighthouse
N
0 1 2
Scale in miles
Vineyard Haven
Oak Bluffs
Nantucket Sound
Tisbury
Vineyard Sound
Cape Poge Lighthouse
Edgartown Lighthouse
Edgartown
West Tisbury
Chappaquidick Island
Gay Head Lighthouse
Chilmark
Menemsha
Aquinnah (Gay Head)
Atlantic Ocean

Vineyard Places

OAK BLUFFS

LOCATED ON THE NORTH SIDE OF MARTHA'S VINEYARD, Oak Bluffs was originally settled as Wesleyan Grove in 1835. It served as the site for Methodist revival meetings that soon attracted other religious groups. Attendees first pitched tents for the duration of the event, but later built wood structures. Those seasonal houses evolved into more elaborately decorated cottages that provided inspiration for the many gingerbread-style homes that now distinguish the town. To complement the architectural style, the town was renamed Cottage City when it was incorporated in 1880. By 1907, because it could no longer be considered a "cottage" city, the town was renamed Oak Bluffs.

Though the revival meetings still take place, Oak Bluffs is now also appreciated for its secular tourist attractions such as hiking, dining, and shopping. It claims the largest marina on Martha's Vineyard and one of the oldest operating carousels in the United States.

Surrounded by neat rows of gingerbread houses, the gazebo in Ocean Park overlooking Nantucket Sound is one of visitors' first sights when arriving by ferry in Oak Bluffs. The park faces north, giving it a view of Nantucket Sound and the Atlantic Ocean. This area of Oak Bluffs is lined with gingerbread houses. What distinguishes a gingerbread house from other Queen Ann–style designs is the finely cut trim work and decorative siding. The intricately carved trim and bright colors are truly similar to cleverly frosted sheets of gingerbread. Popular toward the end of the 19th century, during Queen Victoria's reign, Queen Ann–style architecture is characterized by the inclusion of gables, dormers, towers, and even turrets. The decorative trim, porch posts, and spindles with lacy cutouts that make up the "gingerbread" are also typical, but not a defining Queen Ann feature. The patterned or "fishscale" shingles also add to the gingerbread appearance.

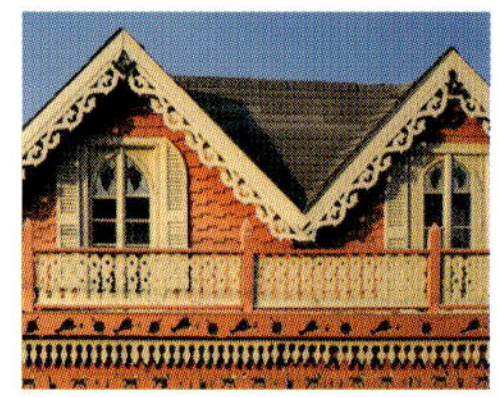

Page 14

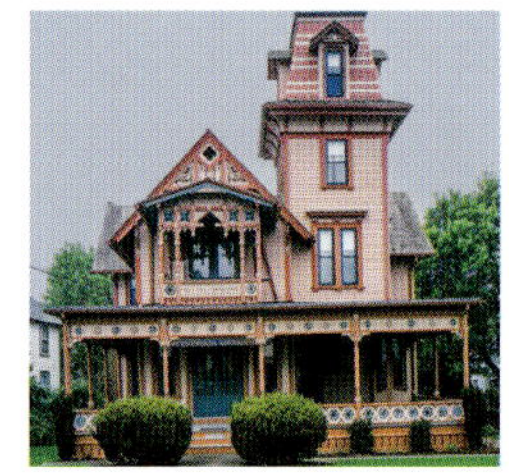

Page 16

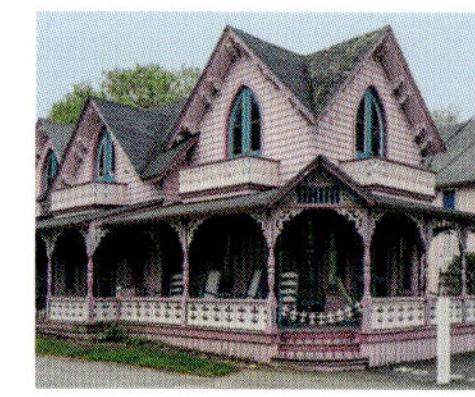

Page 17

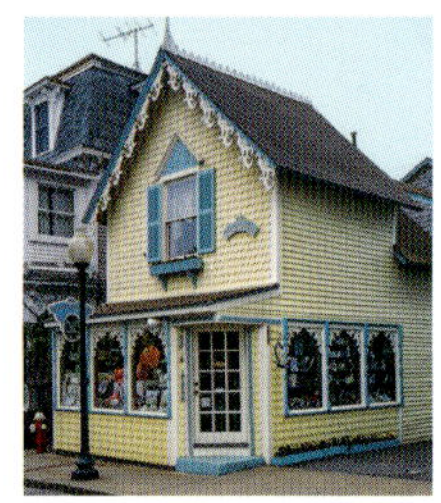

Page 18

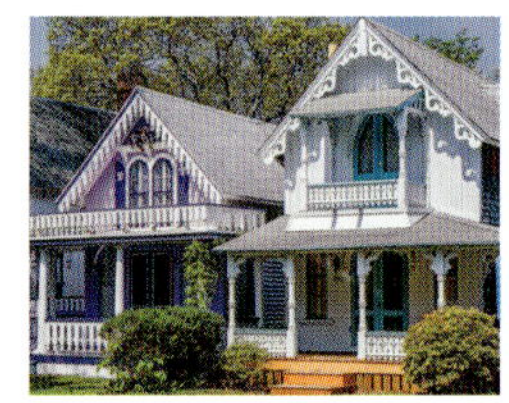

Page 19

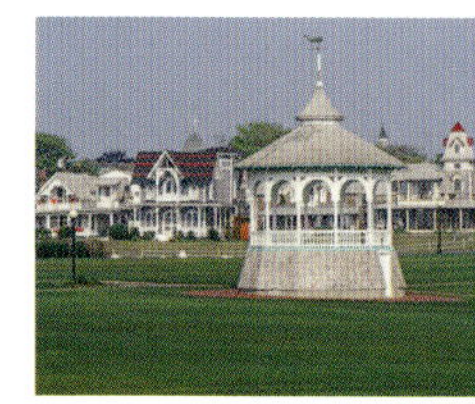

Page 20

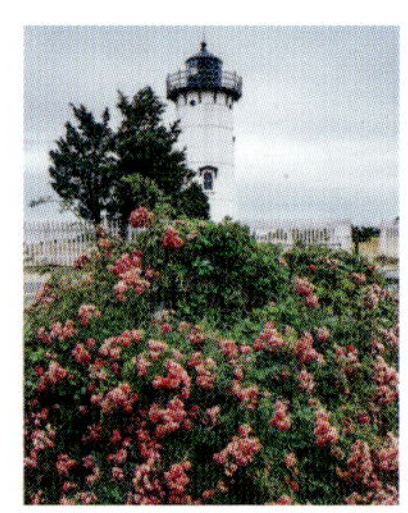

Page 21

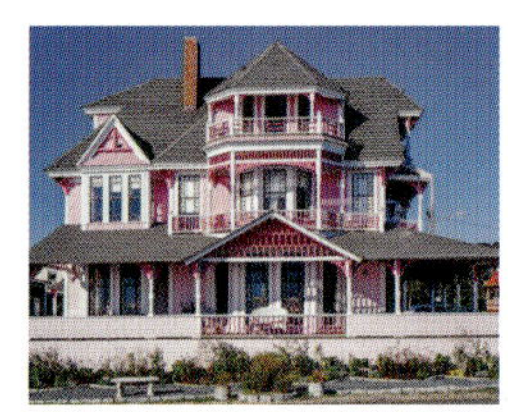

Page 34

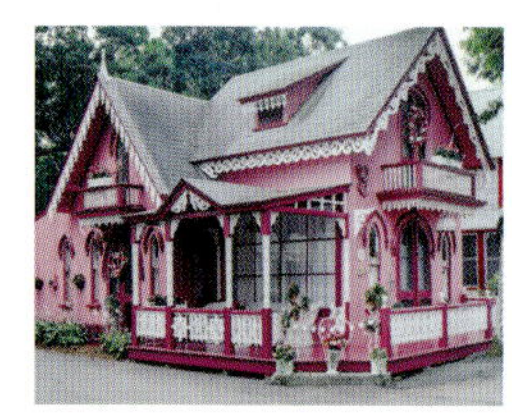

Page 35

EDGARTOWN

SETTLED IN 1641, AND THE ADMINISTRATIVE SEAT OF Dukes County since 1642, Edgartown was Martha's Vineyard's first settlement. Edgartown captures much of the spirit of Martha's Vineyard with its combination of whaling history and modern tourist attractions. Home to Edgartown Lighthouse, the town overlooks Nantucket Sound. It offers a view of Chappaquiddick across Katama Bay and access to five beaches. Museums such as the Vincent House, the oldest home on Martha's Vineyard, and the Old Whaling Church bespeak the history waiting to be rediscovered in this community.

The Greek-revival style, clapboard-fronted buildings along North Water Street are fastidiously maintained historic homes of 19th-century whaling captains. Some houses are even older. In the yards of these homes and throughout Edgartown, the landscaping is consistently breathtaking. The houses overlook a wharf that has been in use for hundreds of years. The entire area preserves a New England heritage of shipping, fishing, and whaling.

In addition to its long history, Edgartown enjoys its share of modern commercial activity on the Vineyard. It's a charming tourist town with large hotels, fine dining, and shopping. There are also beaches and preserved lands that invite visitors to the great outdoors.

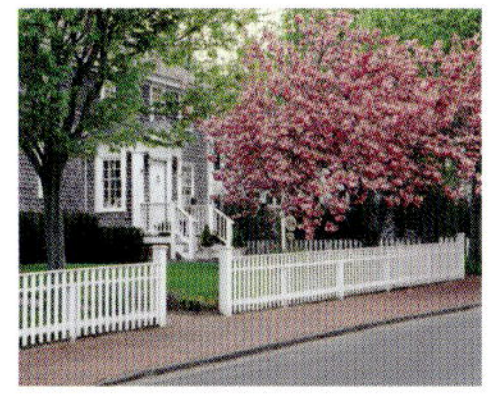

Page 25

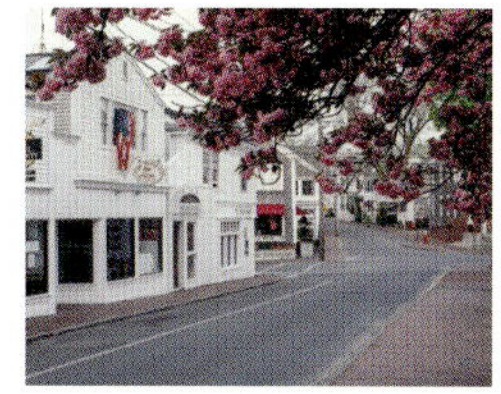

Page 26

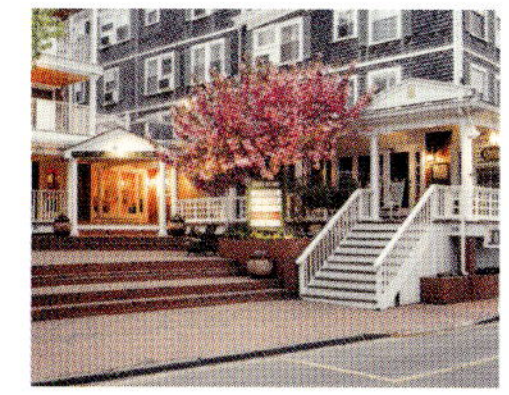

Page 27

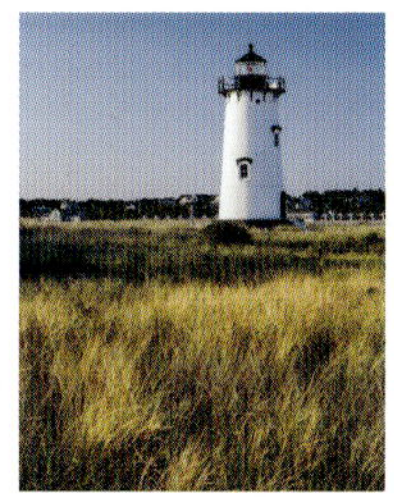

Page 36

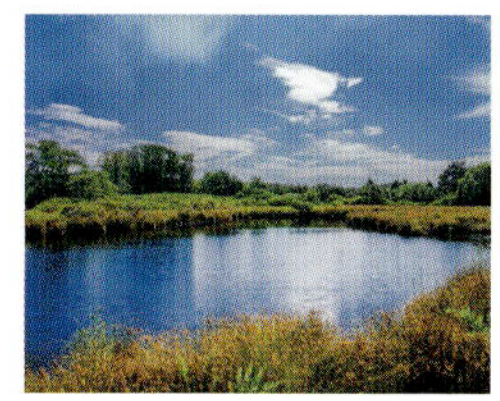

Page 37

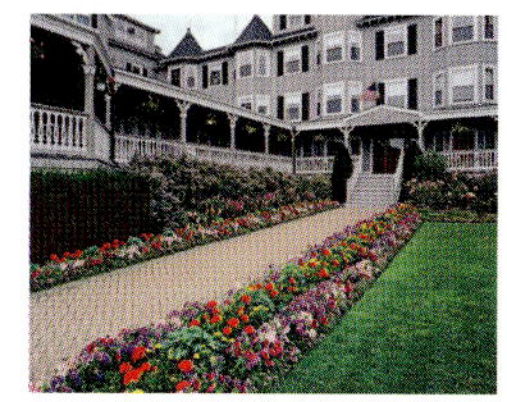

Page 38

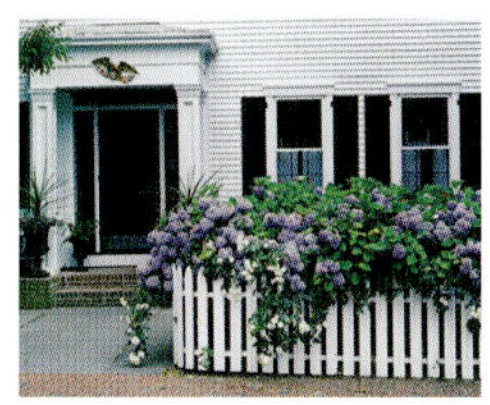

Page 39

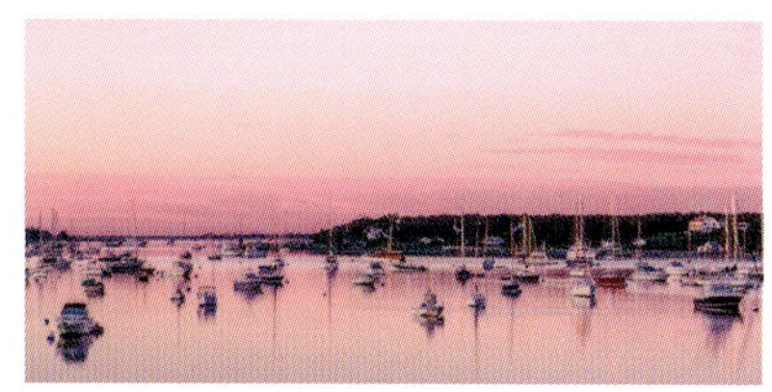

Page 40

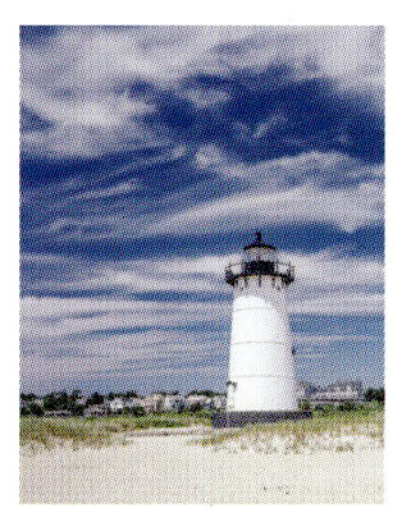

Page 41

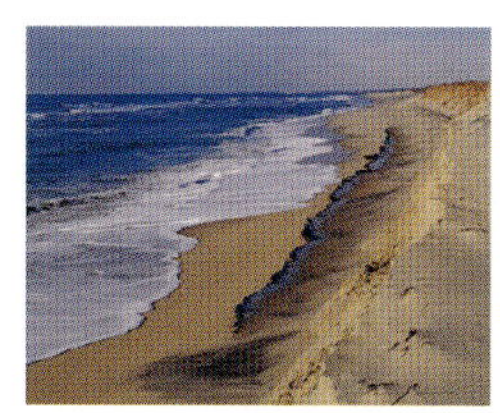

Page 59

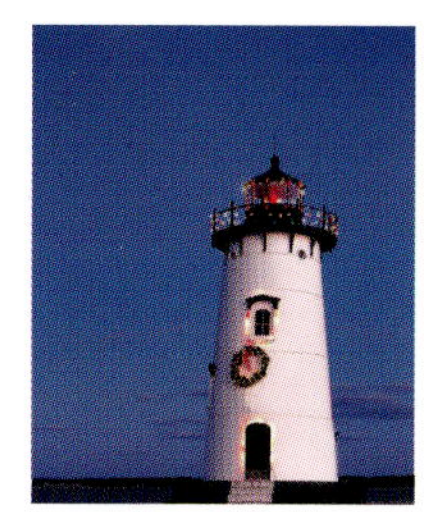

Page 65

CHAPPAQUIDDICK

CONNECTED TO MARTHA'S VINEYARD BY A NARROW barrier beach on the south side of Edgartown across Katama Bay, Chappaquiddick is part of Edgartown, but also a separate island that can be reached by ferry. The barrier beach road is closed to public traffic. The island was named for the Chappaquiddick, one of four native peoples who lived on Martha's Vineyard.

Chappaquiddick is home to a number of natural, preserved lands, including (1) Brine's Pond, with more than 40 acres of wetlands, forest, and hiking trails; (2) Chappy Five Corners, with 27 acres of pine-oak forest; (3) Chappy Point Beach, which includes some 700 feet of beachfront; (4) North Neck Highlands Preserve, a wildlife refuge; (5) Poucha Pond, almost 100 acres of forests and salt marsh; and (6) the Wasque Reservation.

In addition, Chappaquiddick contains Cape Poge Wildlife Refuge, which covers more than 500 acres of bird habitat and is managed by The Trustees of Reservations.

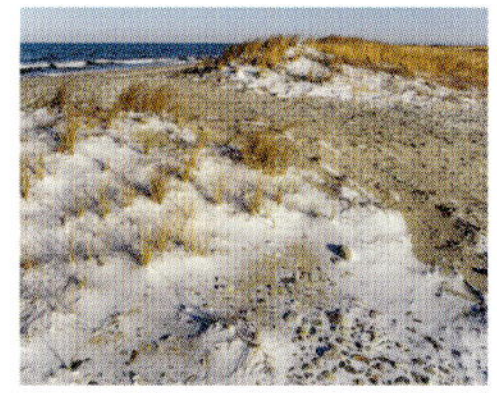

Page viii

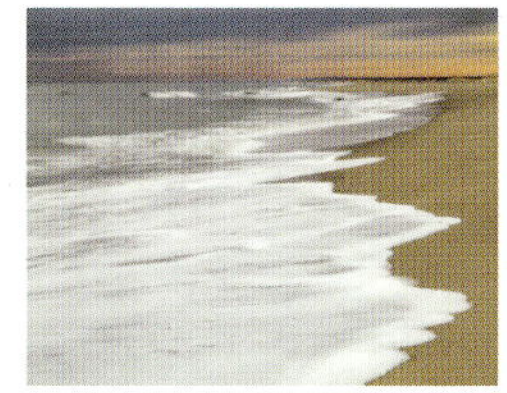

Page 2

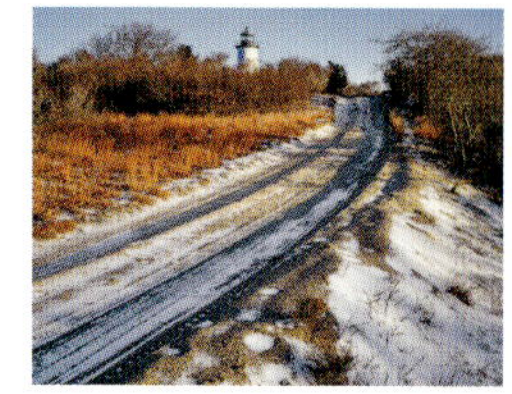

Page 3

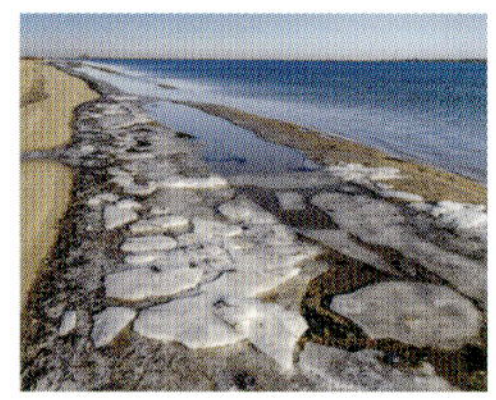

Page 4

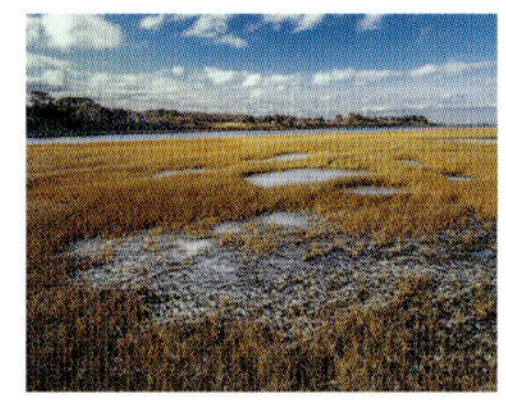

Page 6

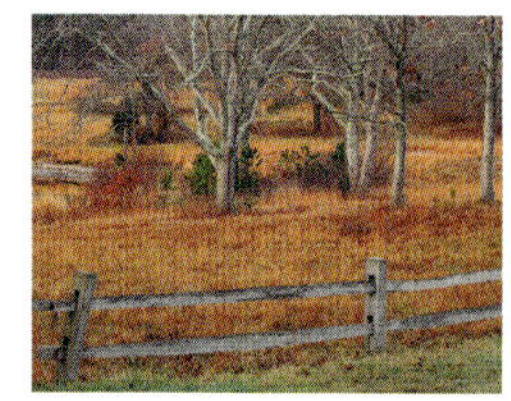

Page 7

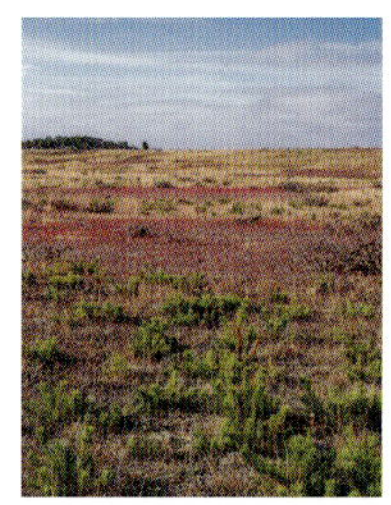

Page 12

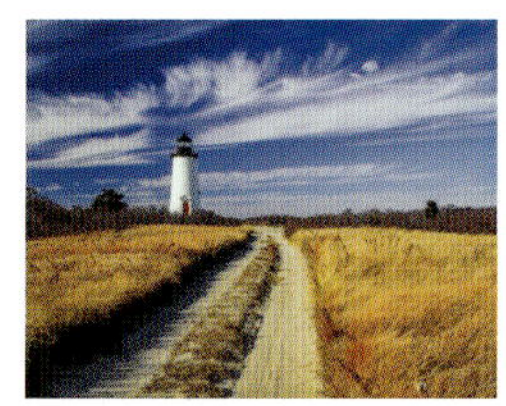

Page 57

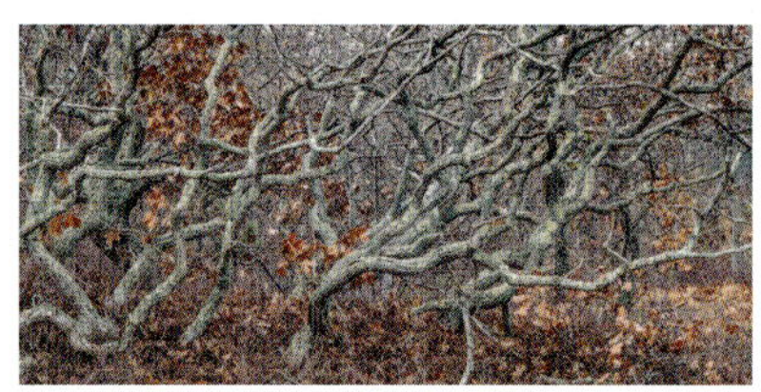

Page 64

WEST TISBURY

LOCATED ON THE WESTERN SIDE OF MARTHA'S VINEYARD and southwest of Tisbury, West Tisbury is the agricultural center of the island. It was settled in 1669, and originally named Takemmy, which means "where anybody goes to grind corn." West Tisbury boasted a gristmill, an amenity that was unavailable in towns that lacked a river or stream for power. Downtown West Tisbury is home to a farmers' market and the Agricultural Hall, both of which are testaments to the town's farming heritage. West Tisbury was part of Tisbury until 1892, when it was incorporated in its own right.

West Tisbury's contribution to the whaling industry was the production of satinet, a wool fabric used in sailor's gear. Whaling captains adopted the town, too, and Music Street is still lined with their homes.

West Tisbury is also known for natural woodlands and beaches. Cedar Tree Neck Preserve is a wetlands preserve entrusted to the Sheriff's Meadow Foundation, which was founded in 1959 to preserve lands on the island. Also in West Tisbury is the oak forest of Long Point Wildlife Refuge. Part of more than 23,000 acres of properties in Massachusetts managed by The Trustees of Reservations, the refuge is home to many rare species of wildlife in a variety of habitats, including scrub oak shrublands, sand plain grasslands, coastal heaths, and pine forests.

The Christiantown Memorial marks the site of services held for members of the Wampanoag population who converted to Christianity.

Though they are on the southern part of the island, West Tisbury, Chilmark, and Aquinnah are considered "up island," an expression that refers more to the height above sea level than a location.

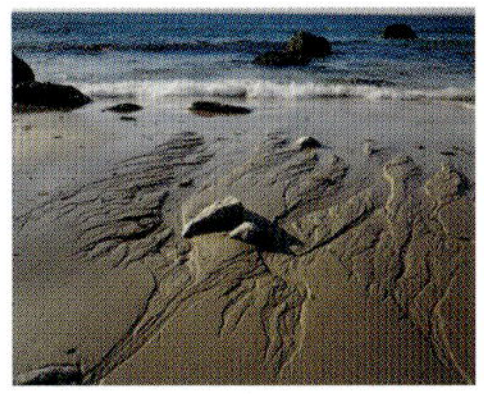

Page 5

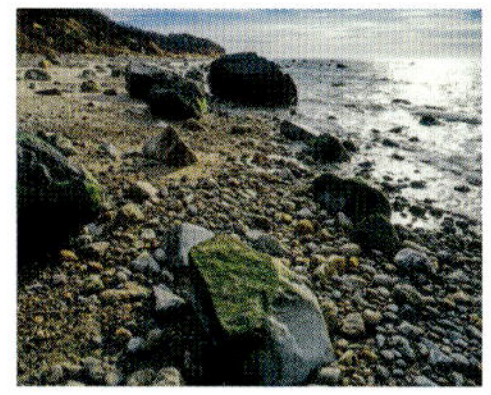

Page 8

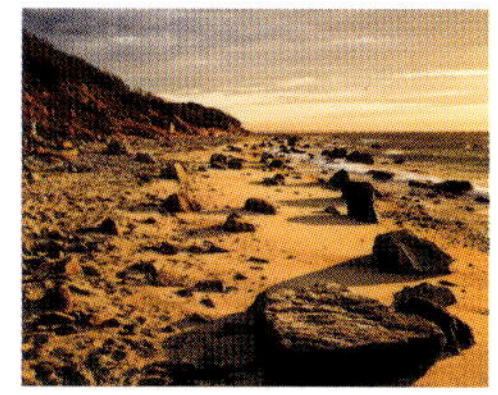

Page 13

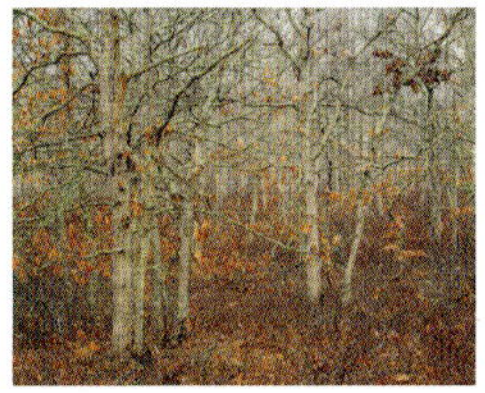

Page 50

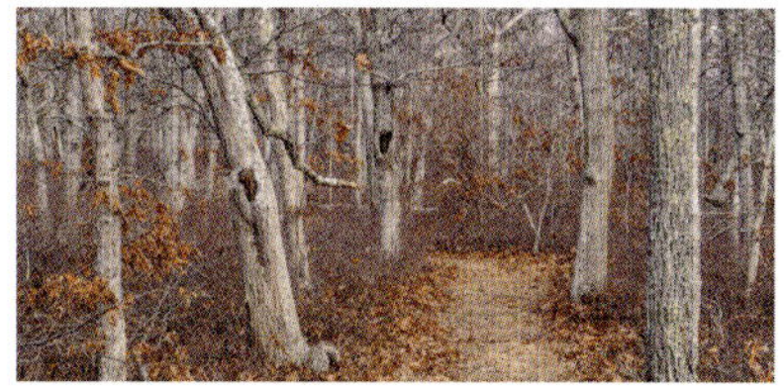

Page 54

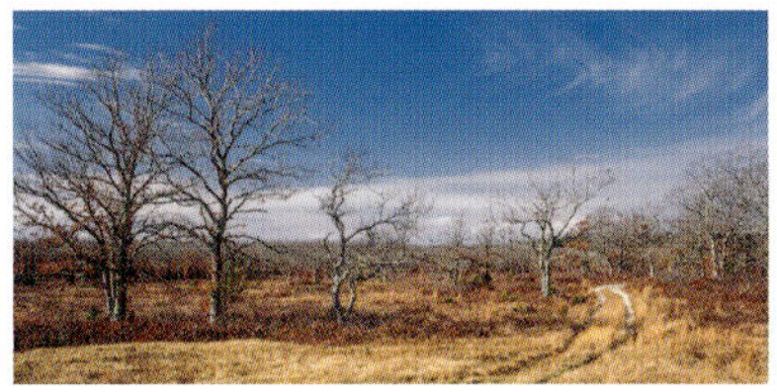

Page 55

CHILMARK & MENEMSHA

KNOWN AS AN AGRICULTURAL COMMUNITY, CHILMARK was originally settled in the mid-17th century by John Mayhew, the grandson of patentee and island governor Thomas Mayhew. First called Tisbury Manor, the community was incorporated as Chilmark in 1714. At that time it included No Man's Land and the Elizabeth Islands, which are now the town of No Man's Land.

Native Americans called the area "Nashowakemmuck," Algonquian for halfway house. The name "Chilmark" is borrowed from the parish in England where Governor Mayhew's wife originally lived. It replaced Tisbury Manor, a name that people connected with the towns of Tisbury and West Tisbury.

Part of Chilmark, Menemsha is in the southwestern part of the town, just across Menemsha Pond from Aquinnah. Once called Creekville, then Menemsha Creek, its location along Vineyard Sound makes it an ideal lobstering village, with fresh seafood available from vendors. The busy harbor is also home to a U.S. Coast Guard station.

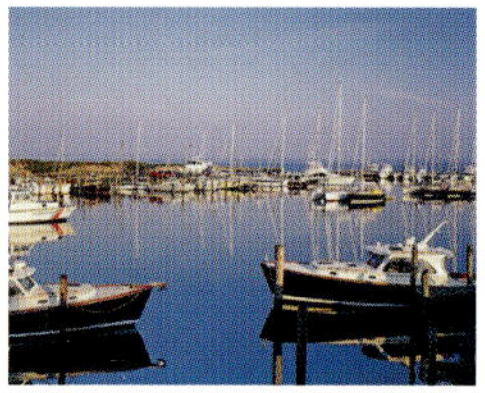

Page 44

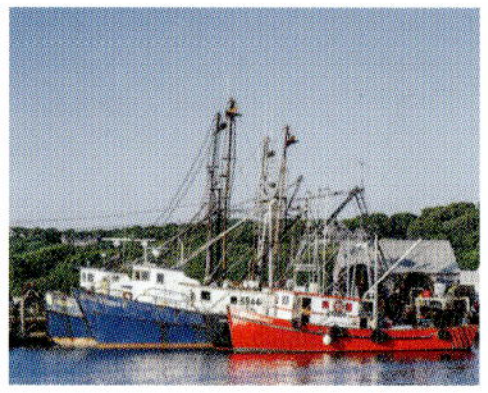

Page 45

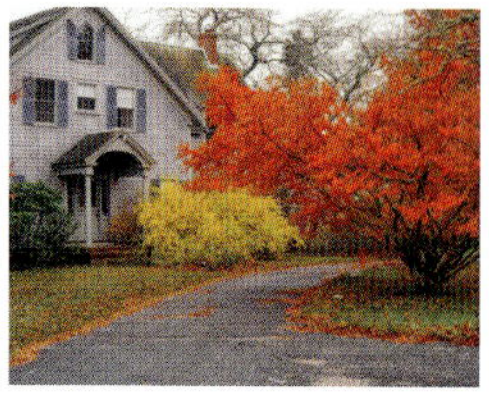

Page 52

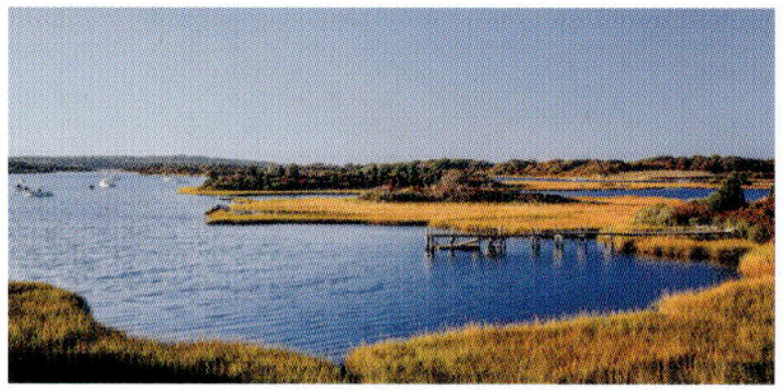

Page 53

AQUINNAH

PREVIOUSLY KNOWN AS GAY HEAD, AQUINNAH WAS renamed in 1998 with the Wampanoag term for "land beneath the hill." By any name, the striking cliffs located on the western tip of Martha's Vineyard were the first sight of home for whalers and other mariners for centuries. Martha's Vineyard was created as a result of glacial movement 10,000 years ago. Named by British sailors, the Gay Head Cliffs are the highest point on the island. Formed by the movements of glaciers and tidal waters, they present an impressively colorful display of ancient layers of sand, gravel, clay, and plant life.

The Gay Head Cliffs provide a view over Vineyard Sound toward No Man's Land. A natural location for a lighthouse, the cliffs support Gay Head Light, which marks the island for eastbound mariners.

Aquinnah Beach actually encompasses four beaches near Gay Head Cliffs. Aquinnah and Moshup are open to the public. In combination they were ranked by a Travel Channel survey as one of the country's top ten beaches overall, and the best walking beach in the country. Philbin and Zack's Cliffs beaches are both private.

In 1987, 485 acres in Aquinnah were designated Tribal Lands, and some 300 of these acres were recognized as common lands that include the Gay Head Cliffs, Herring Creek, and Lobsterville. The cliffs are open to the public, and island tours include a stop there, but to protect them from decay, visitors are asked not to climb the cliffs or remove any materials.

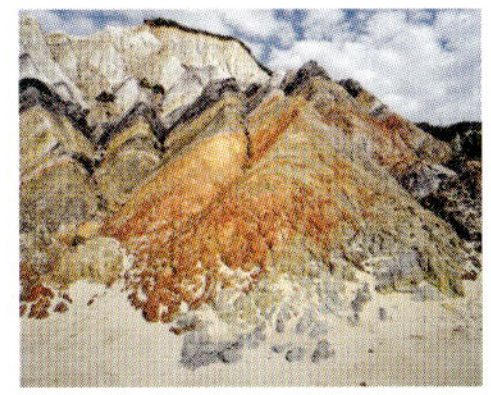

Page iv

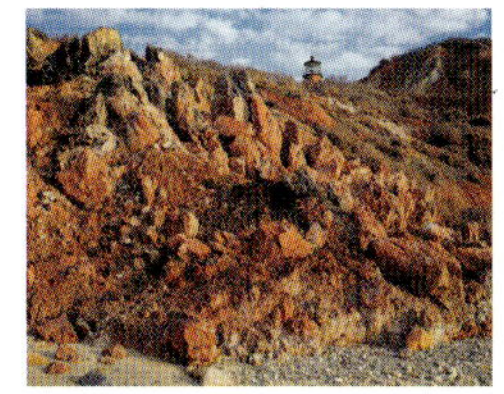

Page 9

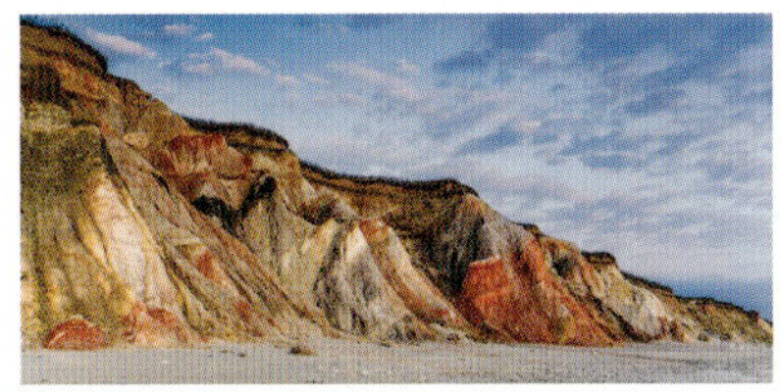

Page 10

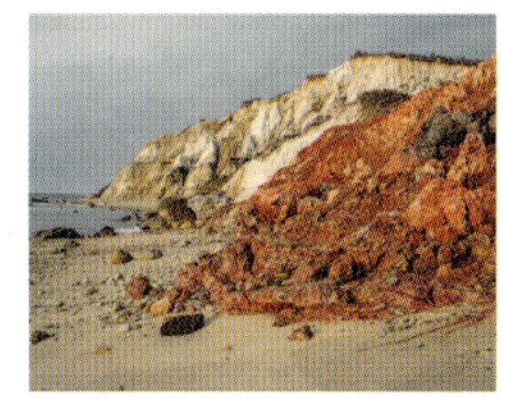

Page 29

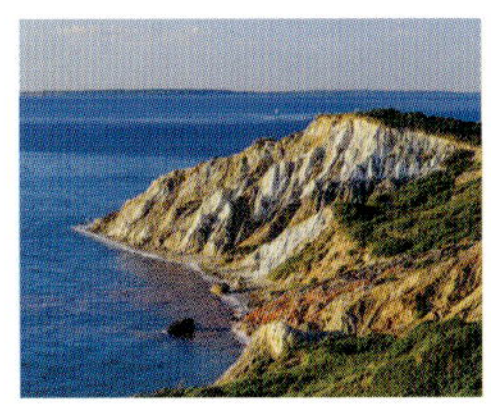

Page 30

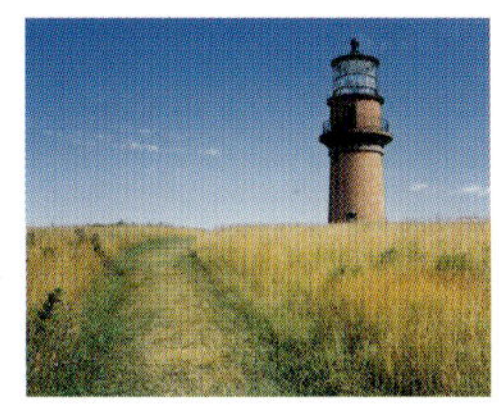

Page 46

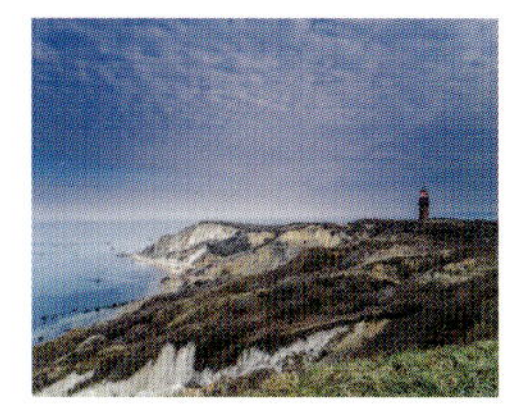

Page 60

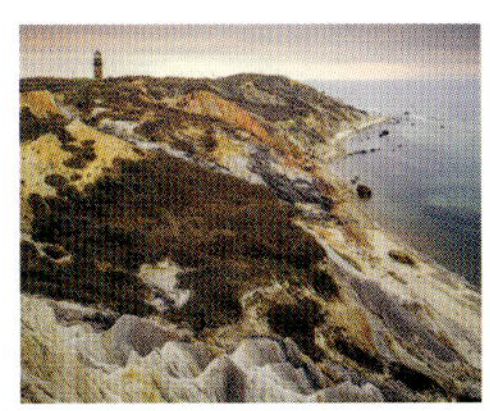

Page 61

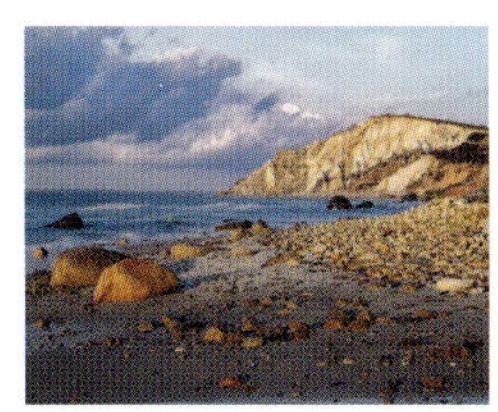

Page 62

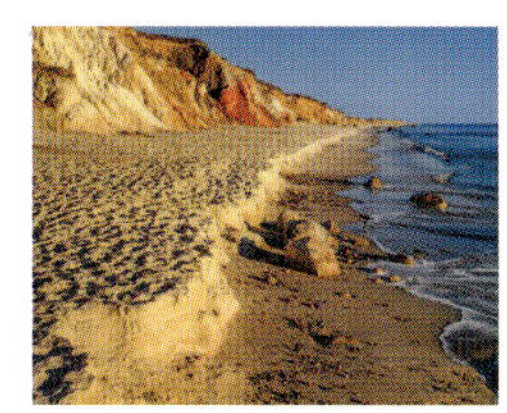

Page 63

TISBURY & VINEYARD HAVEN HARBOR

ALSO KNOWN AS VINEYARD HAVEN, TISBURY IS LOcated on the very northern tip of Martha's Vineyard just across the harbor from Oak Bluffs. When marine shipping routes passed through Vineyard Sound in the early 19th century, Vineyard Haven Harbor was one of the busiest harbors in New England.

The town was originally called Holmes Hole, named after a local landowner and the "hole" or notch in the coastline to which he lent his name. The town was renamed Vineyard Haven, but that designation really applies only to the harbor area. Tisbury, the larger town around the settlement, is the official name for the township, which was incorporated in 1671.

Moored in Vineyard Haven Harbor, the schooners *Shenandoah* and *Alabama* are always a dramatic sight for visitors. The topsail schooner *Shenandoah*, measuring 108 feet on her waterline, was built in 1964, employing shipbuilding practices of the mid-19th century, when similar vessels sailed the Vineyard Sound. She is the only schooner of her size and rig without auxiliary power sailing under the U.S. flag. She sleeps 30 and carries a nine-member crew. The *Alabama*, a 90-foot-long, gaff-rigged schooner, was built in 1926, and underwent a complete re-fitting in 1997. She sleeps 27 and has a crew of six. Both vessels offer weeklong "kids' cruises" where young people can experience and learn every facet of traditional sailing.

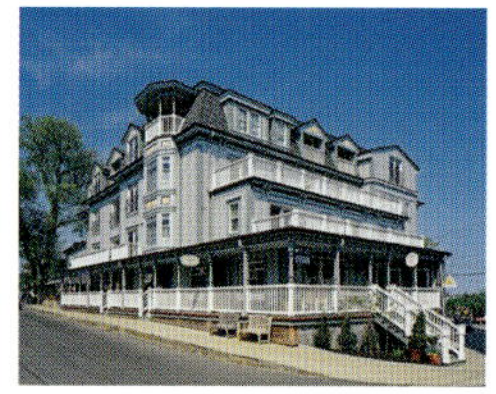
Page 22

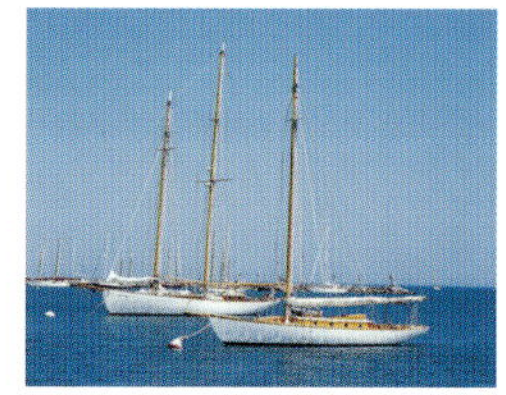
Page 23

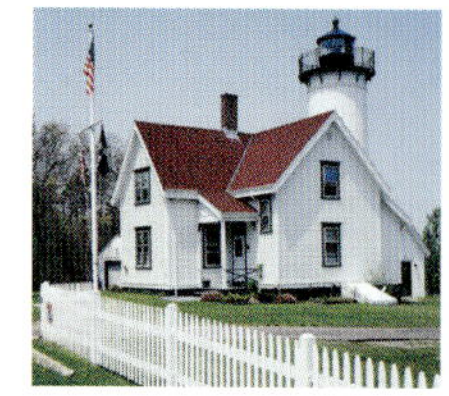
Page 24

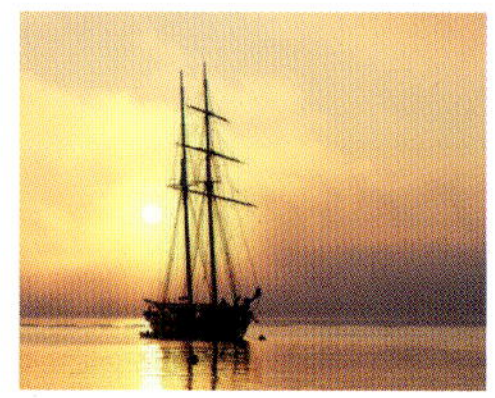
Page 28

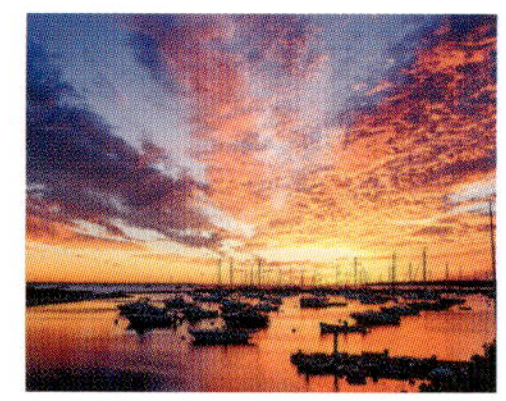
Page 32

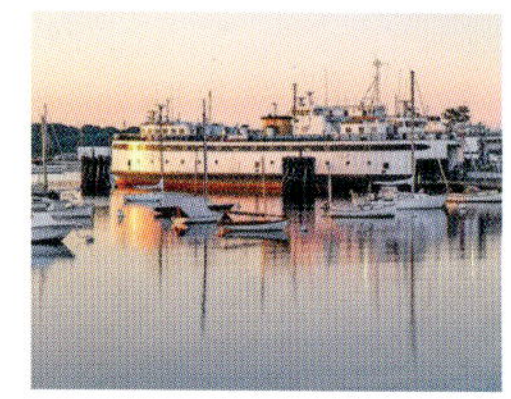
Page 33

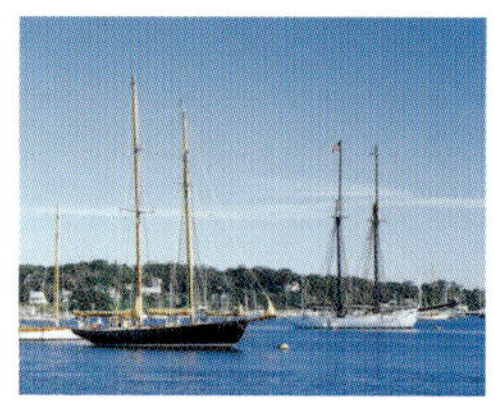
Page 42

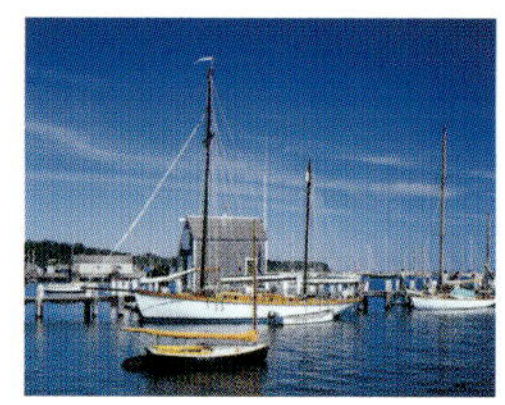
Page 43

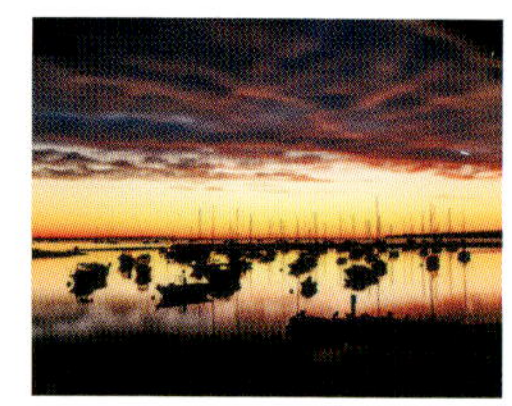
Page 47

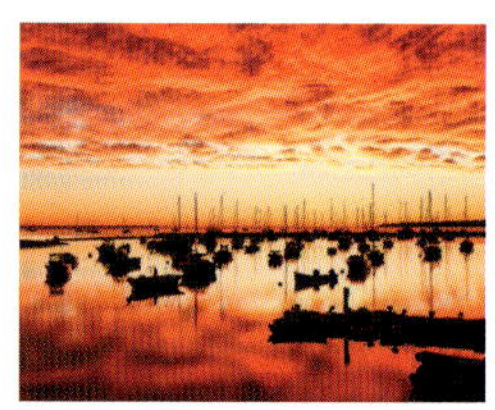
Page 48

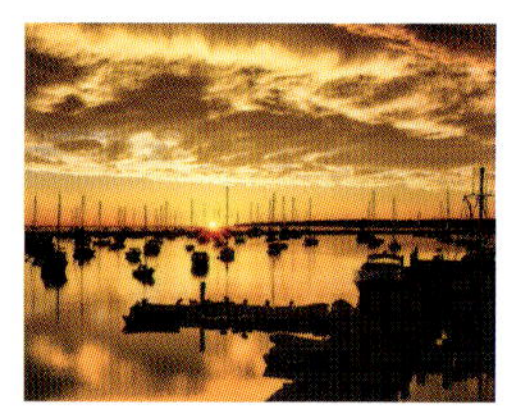
Page 49

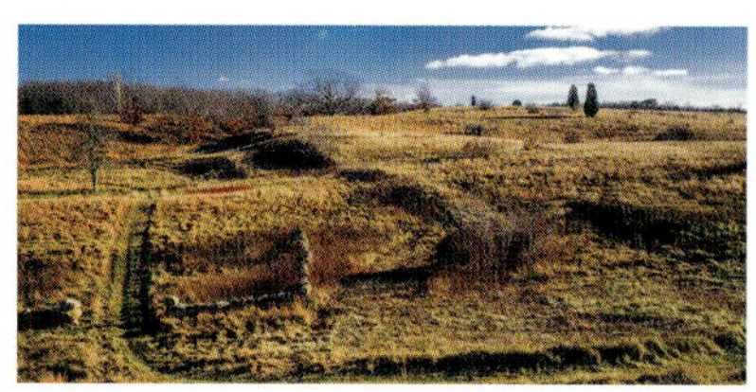
Page 56

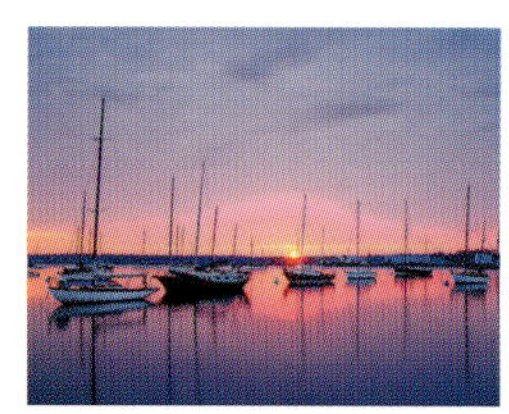
Page 58

The Lighthouses

CAPE POGE LIGHT

Cape Poge Light was first established in 1801 at a time when the islands south of the Massachusetts mainland were busy with whaling vessels, fishing schooners, and freight shipping. The light warned mariners away from Cape Poge and the surrounding sand bars at the tip of Chappaquiddick Island.

The location of the lighthouse proved to be dangerous because of heavy seas and the changing shoreline. Consisting of a wooden structure and a small cottage, the first light was destroyed by the sea in 1838. The second was built farther inland, but it collapsed 50 years later, after the ocean eroded the sand around its base. The third light, a 33-foot tower built in 1892, lasted 35 years. The fourth and current light is a white, wooden, 55-foot tower built in 1922. To preclude destruction, it has been moved several times, once by helicopter!

The 1857 fourth-order Fresnel lens has been replaced by a 300-mm, solar-powered optic that shines at 65 feet above sea level. It is an active aid to navigation, operated by the U.S. Coast Guard under a lease from The Trustees of Reservations.

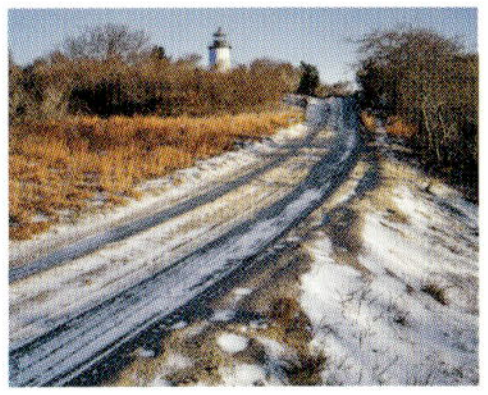

Page 3

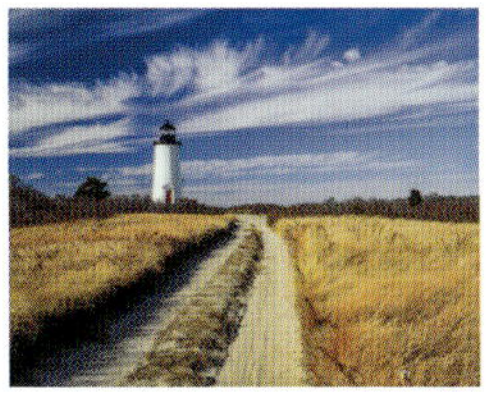

Page 57

EAST CHOP LIGHT

Established in 1869, East Chop Light marks the entrance to Vineyard Haven Harbor from the Oak Bluffs side. Sitting atop Telegraph Hill, the lighthouse is located on the site of one of the first telegraph stations in New England. Signals were exchanged there with stations in Nantucket, Woods Hole, Bonniedale, South Plymouth, and other Massachusetts cities starting in 1828. The original system consisted of a private station, and mariners had to pay to use the service when they entered the area. This was not a popular system, and the station was out of business by 1875.

In 1877, the U.S. government purchased the land and built a 40-foot, sparkplug lighthouse. Eventually, the 1877 Gothic-revival style keeper's quarters were removed, but the 300-mm optic shines at 79 feet above sea level and serves as an active aid to navigation. It is owned by the Martha's Vineyard Historical Society, but is operated by the U.S. Coast Guard.

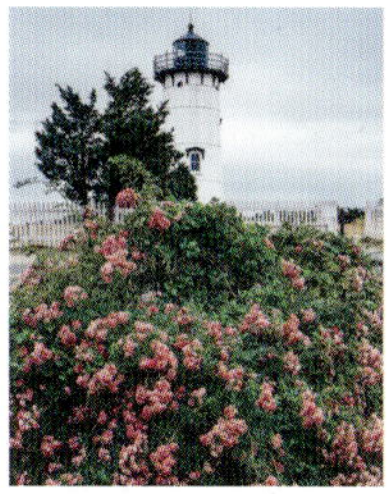

Page 21

EDGARTOWN HARBOR LIGHT

Edgartown Harbor Light was first established in 1828 to mark Edgartown Harbor on the eastern end of Martha's Vineyard. The original Cape Cod–style building with a lantern sat on a small, man-made island a quarter of a mile from shore. A bridge was put in, but destroyed several times. Eventually sand filled in the distance between the shoreline and the island. The first station was destroyed by a hurricane in 1938.

A replacement tower was moved to Edgartown from Crane's Beach, near Ipswich, Massachusetts, in 1939. It is 45 feet tall and shines at 45 feet above sea level. Automated in 1939 after being erected on this site, the 1856 fourth-order Fresnel lens was replaced in 1988 with a 250-mm solar-powered optic that still provides guidance to mariners. The station is owned by the Martha's Vineyard Historical Society but operated by the U.S. Coast Guard.

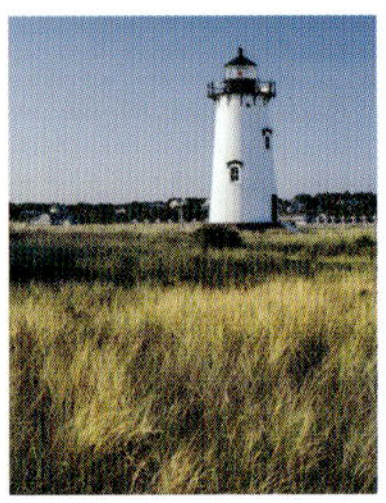

Page 36

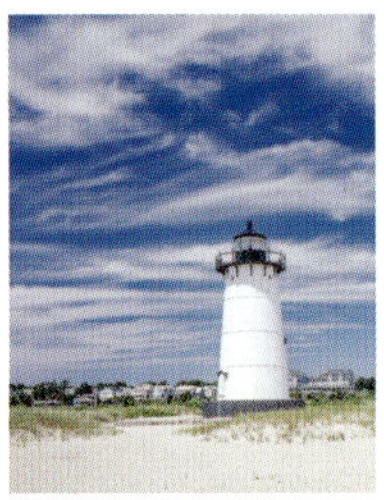

Page 41

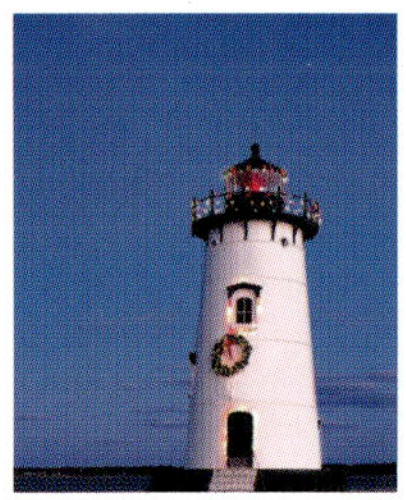

Page 65

GAY HEAD LIGHT

Built by order of President John Quincy Adams in 1799, the station on Gay Head Cliffs marks the western tip of Martha's Vineyard. It was originally a simple wooden tower with lanterns. Its replacement, the current 1856 stone tower, was fitted with an innovative, for the time, first-order Fresnel lens, now housed at the Dukes County Historical Museum. The 1902 keeper's quarters no longer stand.

Seen from the beach below, Gay Head Light appears to be peeking out over the bluff. In reality, its 51-foot tower shines at 170 feet above sea level. Mariners know it by a 15-second alternating pattern of red and white lights.

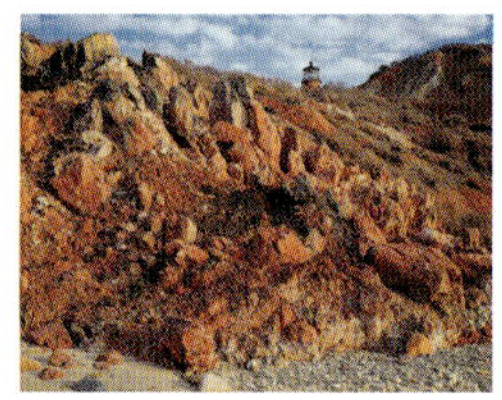

Page 9

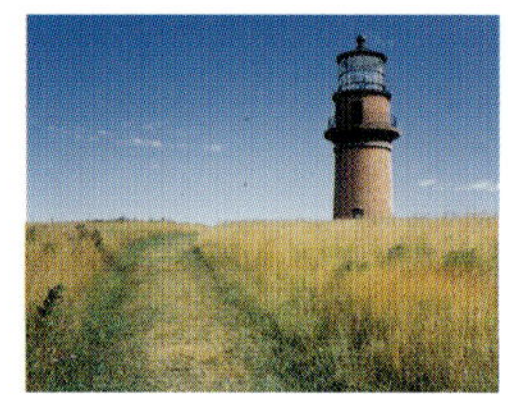

Page 46

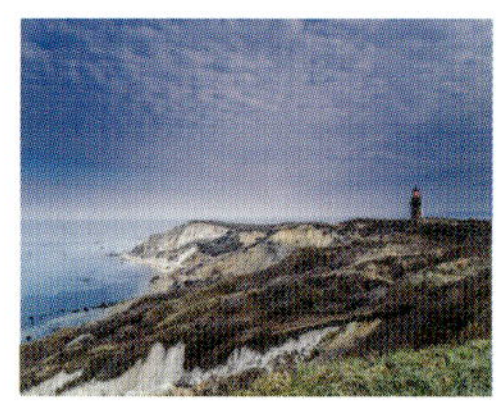

Page 60

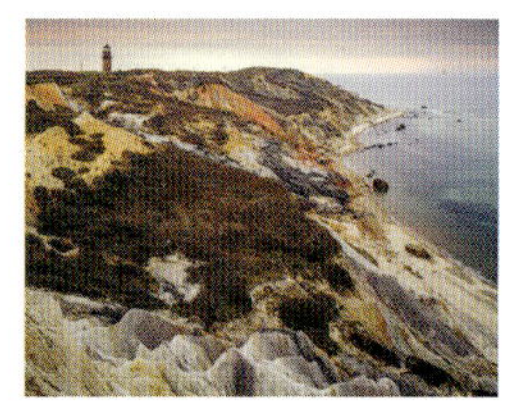

Page 61

WEST CHOP LIGHT

As the ferry from Woods Hole approaches Martha's Vineyard, one of the first features passengers see is West Chop Light, located at the very northern outcropping of Tisbury. Marking Vineyard Haven Harbor, which has served as an important port from as early as 1645, West Chop Light was constructed in 1818.

In 1838 a brick tower with a conical shape replaced the original stone structure. That tower was moved back from shore at least once to protect it from erosion. In 1891 it was replaced by a new tower set even farther away from the shore.

The 52-foot tower seen today shines at 84 feet above sea level and is equipped with a fourth-order Fresnel lens. The Cape Cod fog signal built in 1881 still stands, as do the Victorian-style keeper's quarters dating to 1847. There is also a garage, a storage building, and an oil house.

Automated in 1976, the light remains an active aid to navigation and is owned by the Vineyard Environmental Research Institute.

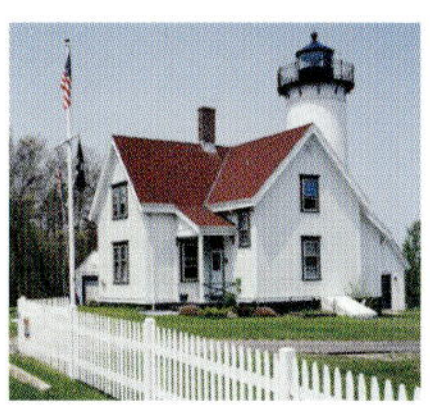

Page 24

Index

About the Photographer

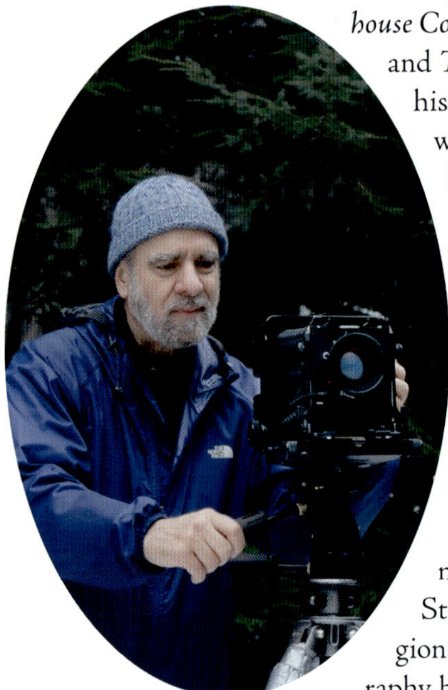

Paul Rezendes is the photographer of Tide-mark's "Lighthouse Companion Series," including *The Lighthouse Companion for Long Island Sound; The Lighthouse Companion for Massachusetts, Rhode Island, and New Hampshire;* and *The Lighthouse Companion for Maine.* Each book features brief histories and full-color photographs of each state's lighthouses, as well as contact information, directions to reach the lighthouses by car, and latitude and longitude to reach them by sea. Appendices cover lodging, local events, and sites of interest.

Rezendes's other books include the highly acclaimed guide *Tracking & the Art of Seeing: How to Read Animal Tracks and Sign; Wetlands: The Web of Life,* coauthored with his wife, Paulette M. Roy; and *The Wild Within: Adventures in Nature and Animal Teachings.* His photographs have appeared in hundreds of calendars, magazines, books, and catalogs; on posters and cards; and in brochures and promotional materials for corporate and commercial accounts in the United States and abroad. He has worked on assignment for several regional and national magazines, and operates his own stock photography business. A native New Englander, Paul grew up in Westport, Massachusetts, and lives with his wife in a remote forest on the banks of the Millers River in Athol, Massachusetts.

Prints for Framing

The photographs in this book are available as high-quality, fine art prints, reproduced on the finest archival photographic papers. Signed upon request. Sizes range from 11" x 14" to 40" x 50". Prices begin at $175 (prints only).

For more information and to order, please contact:

Paul Rezendes Photography
3833 Bearsden Road
Royalston, MA 01368-9400
USA

Tel: **978-249-8810**
e-mail: **photos@paulrezendes.com**
Website: **www.paulrezendes.com**